PIAGETIAN REASONING AND THE BLIND

Yvette Hatwell
University of Grenoble, France

English Edition of
PRIVATION SENSORIELLE ET INTELLIGENCE
with a new Introduction by the author

for the
English Edition
Editor: Beth Stephens
Translator: Pierre Verdet

AMERICAN FOUNDATION FOR THE BLIND

AFB has worked since 1921—with Helen Keller as the Foundation's primary counselor from 1924 until her death in 1968—to improve the quality of life for blind and visually impaired persons.

Today AFB provides national and regional research, consultation, conferences, publications, films, slides, audio and video tapes in the areas of early childhood, education, employment, low vision, rehabilitation and independent living, recreation and leisure, technology, and aging.

The text, and the 1966 introduction and preface, were first published in French, as *Privation sensorielle et intelligence,* in 1966. The French edition is copyright ©1966 by Presses Universitaires de France, Paris.

Library of Congress Cataloging in Publication Data
Hatwell, Yvette
    Piagetian reasoning and the blind.

    Translation of: Privation sensorielle et intelligence.
    Includes bibliographies.
    1. Piaget, Jean, 1896–1980. 2. Cognition in children. 3. Reasoning in children. 4. Visual perception in children. 5. Children, Blind—Intelligence levels.
I. Stephens, Beth. II. Title.

BF723.C5H4213   1985   155.4'511   84–450

ISBN 0–89128–122–3

Printed in the United States of America

Table of Contents

Introduction to the English Edition, 1984

This book was first published in French in 1966. In it were reported the results of a set of research projects I had undertaken in the early 1960s concerning the cognitive development of children affected by congenital blindness. My main interest was to establish if—and how—early blindness affected the achievement of the concrete operational thinking at the heart of Piagetian theory.

I believe that at the time of its publication there had been no other work on this subject; since 1966, a good deal of research has been devoted to the study of the impact of early visual deprivation on the development of logical thinking, particularly in the U.S. and Great Britain.

I welcome this English translation of my book: by lifting the language barrier I hope it will inspire more young English-speaking researchers to delve into this subject. Also, I am sure it will facilitate comparison of my early findings with those subsequently published in the English language.

As two decades have elapsed since publication of this work, I feel that it is now appropriate to make several comments, mainly in two areas:

1. *From a theoretical standpoint,* the scientific context which prevailed when my experimental work was in progress (in particular the context of Piaget's theory) has undergone a substantial evolution in recent years. Unless the reader is fully aware of these changes the methodology adopted and some results may lose their full significance. Therefore the question of the validity of my conclusions vis-a-vis today's theories must be addressed.

2. *From the experimental standpoint,* many new results have been generated by others, results which necessarily affect my conclusions. Authors have discussed my work and formulated objections. It would be unfair to miss this opportunity to discuss and respond.

I shall therefore address these two issues in the following comments:

Congenitally Blind (CB) Children's Performance and Piagetian Theory

Chapter II summarizes the state of Piaget's theory in the middle 1960s. In those years, Piaget's approach was predominantly structural: the emphasis was put on the logical components of the four main stages describing the child's reasoning from birth to adulthood, and their hierarchical organization. The transition from one stage to the next was conceived as the result of interactions between the subject and his environment through a dynamic process called "equilibration" (between assimilation and accommodation). Although Piaget's epistemology was already typically interactionist (rejecting both purely nativist and purely empiricist views), the role of the subject was considered to be nevertheless much more important than that of the object. This appears in Piaget's assumption that assimilation and accommodation do not have the same weight (assimilation is dominant and is the very source of knowledge) and in the corollary assumption that figurative aspects of thinking that concern the accomodative functions of perception and mental imagery are subordinate to operative ones.

In studying the development of concrete operations in CB children, my aim was to reevaluate the role of figurative knowledge in the cognitive functioning of the child. Congenital blindness results in a severe sensory deprivation which may partly be compensated by an intensive use of the haptic modality. Nevertheless, this compensation is always incomplete since the informational capabilities of the visual system are much greater than those of the haptic one. On the other hand, language is—apparently—not affected by blindness, thus preserving abstract and conceptual abilities in blind children.

My reasoning, therefore, was as follows: If perceptual knowledge actually has more importance than is claimed by Piaget, a specific developmental lag should be observed in the CB's achievement of the concrete operational stage. This lag should be more marked in infralogical operations, which involve perceptual organization of concrete objects, while it should be less apparent in verbally presented logico-mathematical tasks. One should keep in mind that the blindness discussed here concerns only blind children who have a normal intellectual development as measured by general intelligence tests.

To test these hypotheses, two sets of comparisons had to be made: (1) an intergroup comparison between the haptic performances of the blind and the visual ones of normally sighted subjects allowed to see (NS); and (2) an intertask comparison between the performances of the CB in the various Piagetian tasks used. Moreover, two additional control groups were tested in some of the experiments reported (but not in all, because of research contingencies): a group of blindfolded sighted (BS) and a group of late blind (LB) subjects.

The analysis of the empirical data led me to the conclusion that the child's performance depends on both his or her visual status and on the nature of the task he or she has to solve, since the predicted interaction between these two factors did in fact occur. Concrete reasoning was achieved in the CB three to five years later than in the NS for infralogical tasks (spatial representation and physical conservation) while the developmental lag of the CB was attenuated in the verbally presented logico-mathematical operations (0-to-2 years of delay). In addition, when tested, BS and LB groups performed more like the NS than like the CB.

1. *As to Piaget's conceptions in the 1960s,* the fact that early visual deprivation (but not late deprivation) so markedly affects the attainment of some concrete operations showed first that a rehabilitation of the role of perceptual figurative knowledge was to some degree necessary. Next, verbal abilities which are preserved in blindness cannot fully compensate for the lack of visual experience as long as infralogical operations are involved. However, and thirdly, the normally developed language of the CB allows them performances similar to those of the sighted in some verbally presented logico-mathematical operations. This signifies

that in the NS (as Piaget and many other observers have stated earlier), concretely presented tasks are easier than verbally presented ones and are therefore achieved earlier, even when the formal structure of the tasks is the same. By contrast, the attainment of both kinds of tasks occurs almost simultaneously in the CB (at about 9-to-11 years of age).

Some of my findings supported Piaget's views, others were at variance with them. For example, the delay observed in the achievement of concrete operations in the CB supports Piaget's claim that logical growth does not stem from linguistic development, since this latter evolves normally in the CB. This fact was emphasized by Piaget and Inhelder (1966) who related it to Furth's work showing that early deaf children are not delayed in attaining the concrete operational stage. But Piaget and Inhelder focused only on this limited aspect of my results and failed to comment on the fact that logical performances of the CB are better in the verbal than in the concrete problems. If, as they claimed, language development depends itself on prior coordination of sensorimotor and concrete operative schemes of actions, how could it be that in the CB, verbal reasoning develops simultaneously and even before reasoning applied to concrete objects? Thus, my work with the blind led me to question Piaget on what he called the "filiation of structures" (this means that a higher structure is generated from a lower one through an integrative process leading to a new level of equilibrium): what was the lower level that had generated the higher verbal operations in the CB, since the corresponding concrete ones were not already achieved?

Therefore, the great variability in the age at which CB children attain the concrete stage showed dramatically how important is the content to which logical structures are to be applied. Changing the perceptual-figurative basis of some tasks (by using CB subjects) while maintaining unchanged the verbal basis of others modifies the age at which these tasks are correctly performed and, as a result, changes the intertask hierarchy of difficulty usually observed in NS children.

2. *Are these questions still valid today* in the face of recent modifications of Piagetian theory? The substantial work done on normal children in the last decade by Piaget and his associates, and by other researchers, has greatly modified cognitive developmental psychology. This is not the place for a lengthy account of this evolution, since full reviews are already available (Bramaud du Boucheron, 1983; Lautrey, 1981; Bullinger and Chatillon, 1983, etc.). I will therefore comment on only three factors that are directly related to the present discussion.

a. Piaget's epistemology underwent significant changes when, in the early 1970s, he conducted, with his Genevan staff, a series of research on the development of causality concepts in children (Piaget and Garcia, 1971). These research led him to revise some of his early ideas concerning subject-object interaction and to attribute to the object a role greater than he had done in the past. Consequently, as far as the effects of the perceptual deprivation resulting from blindness are concerned, my results are definitely easier to interpret in Piaget's contemporary frame of reference than in the 1960's one.

b. Moreover, further research in Europe and in the U.S.A. has shown that a normal child, if tested on varied logical concepts of the concrete stage, does not necessarily attain the same level of achievement in all of them, and the same intra-subject horizontal time shifts or displacements are observed in the transition from the concrete to the formal stage (Longeot, 1978). Other research has evidenced that the same concrete operation (a class inclusion problem, for example) may be successfully performed when applied to a particular content and failed when applied to another having some different connotations in "natural thinking." Lastly, significant individual differences have been observed, leading some authors to search for "cognitive styles" in children's operational abilities. These styles have often been related to the "visual-field-dependence" of Witkin (Huteau, 1980; Ohlmann and Mendelsohn, 1982, etc.).

Thus, studies based on horizontal time shifts, on natural thinking and on cognitive styles have seriously questioned the validity of an exclusively structural approach to cognition: the variability of the age at which the concrete stage is achieved in normal children in the different areas tested has somewhat lowered the value of debating on the filiation of structures, and the problem raised by the CB variability should now be integrated with the wider one of the varied developmental routes leading to adult thinking.

c. In the decade preceding his death in 1980, Piaget himself clearly changed his approach to child intelligence. He was less interested in describing the logical structure of each level; rather, he focused on the study of the psychological processes accounting for the growth of reasoning abilities (Piaget, 1975;1977;1978, etc.). This reorientation was specifically sparked by Inhelder who, following her early work with retardate children (1943), was more interested in the functional analysis of cognition than in its structural description. This functionalistic orientation, already apparent in Inhelder's research on learning (Inhelder et al., 1974), is obvious now in the extensive studies she is conducting with her co-workers on the strategies and procedures used by children to solve a problem (Inhelder et al., 1976; Inhelder and Piaget, 1979).

In conclusion, I believe that if my 1966 Piagetian-oriented work with the blind were to be replicated today, such a replication should not be limited to an evaluation of the blind's operational stages, but rather should be extended to a detailed analysis of the ways by which blind and sighted children solve the same logical problem and of the cues on which each group relies.

Recent Work: Objections and Answers

It is time now to review recent work on operational thinking in the blind in order to see if the developmental lag observed in 1966 has been further confirmed or invalidated. I will first comment on some matters concerning methodology, and then I will review the results obtained by other reseachers.

Many authors have objected to the nature of the sampling of blind subjects in my study. Some of these objections are pertinent, others denote, I am afraid, a misunderstanding of the aim of the research.

Commenting on my experiments on substance conservation, Cromer (1973) listed "several drawbacks" in them, the first being that "no control group of sighted beyond the age of 8" was used and that "the seven- and eight-year-old sighted tested made their judgments while being able to view the material." This comment loses its validity when one recalls that my objective was to assess the mean age at which each task was achieved by the blind and the sighted; since approximately 80 percent of the eight-year-old sighted NS children performed substance conservation correctly, there was no need to test older ones. By contrast, the same 80 percent of successes was achieved only at 12-to-13 years of age in the CB. On the other hand, as stated earlier, the comparison between the *haptic* performances of the CB and the *visual* ones of the sighted was crucial to test the hypotheses concerning the effects of early visual deprivation. While also of interest, the comparison between the CB and the blindfolded sighted (BS) has only a minor significance.

Cromer (1973) objected also that half of the blind subjects were from rural areas, while the sighted had an urban origin. This criticism is valid only up to a point. The "rural" blind children had had some years of life in a great city since they were institutionalized in Paris; they were no longer true "rural scholars," as they had already been exposed to the Parisian sociocultural scene. Furthermore, even if we consider them as true rurals, it is highly improbable that their achievements in substance conservation could be fully accounted for by their social status: I am not aware of any research showing that European rural populations are delayed to such an extent in achieving conservation concepts. Finally, and most importantly, it is a reasoning error to isolate the substance conservation experiment from the rest as reported in 1966: if the rural environment or culture were to be considered responsible for the developmental lag observed in the achievement of conservation in the CB, why did it not play the same negative role in all the tasks tested, especially in the verbal ones whose susceptibility to cultural influences is well known?

To continue with Cromer's objections, he writes: "blind children in Paris begin school two years later than sighted children." Following the same line of thought, Gottesman (1973) writes that "the blind subjects. . .were two-to-three years older than the sighted because in France, they enter school two years later than sighted subjects." These statements reflect a lack of information on the French educational system. There is of course room for improvement, but fortunately, since as early as the 1960s, blind children have entered school as soon as possible, sometimes at the age of three or four years.

There are, however, two real problems that could be of more relevance to Cromer's and Gottesman's interpretations (these problems are introduced and discussed in Chapter III and Chapter VIII): first, to avoid early separation from his family, the blind child is sometimes enrolled first in the *local* non-specialized school and only later (around 7 years) in the Braille school. This may have a negative impact on his schooling. Secondly, urban children schooled very early in Braille actually achieve a grade level generally inferior to that of the sighted having the same chronological age. In my blind sample, the maximum accepted lag in the school level was two years. The reason why I introduced such a difference between blind and sighted samples is that equating the two populations on school achievement necessarily distorts the I.Q. distribution of the blind since blind, since only highly gifted children can learn Braille as quickly as sighted children learn the printed alphabet. These exceptional blind subjects are not representative of the whole congenitally blind population. Consequently, I selected my blind sample only on the basis of an IQ measure (IQ ranging from 80-to-140, with a mean group IQ varying from 98-to-105 in the different experiments). Therefore, blind groups included, in addition to some gifted children who were not delayed in their school achievement, those whose school level was one or two years behind that of the sighted.

This blind population has been compared to sighted children having a school level strictly normal for their chronological age. Such a procedure excluded from the sample retarded children (no IQ measure was available for the sighted) and, contrary to what has been done with blind children, it excluded also very gifted ones. Since this latter bias favors the blind subject, it cannot account for the observed results.

Another factor affecting my control in 1966 was where the children lived: about 60 percent of the blind were institutionalized while the sighted ones lived at home. The relevance of this bias has further been illustrated by Brekke et al. (1974). Studying weight conservation in *legally* blind (including, therefore, subjects who still have useful vision) they observed a significant effect of the place of the residence: institutionalized blind achieved weight conservation later than the blind who lived at home. This factor may therefore partly explain the 1966 results. Nevertheless, it should be remembered that adventitiously blind subjects performed better than the CB although they were institutionalized too. Moreover, even if institutionalization had acted as a handicap, the magnitude of its impact appears to be not the same in all the areas tested. For example, the CBs were not seriously delayed in some logico-mathematical tasks. Again, the intertask comparison leads to a reconsidering of the possible effects of sample biases.

In concluding these methodological considerations, two aspects of my research will be underlined. First, in each of the experiments reported, different age level groups have been tested until at least 50 percent of success was observed in one age group. The number of subjects in each group varied from 10-to-22 with an age range within groups restricted to 12 months (or sometimes 24 months). Testing such large samples of CB is unusual since congenital blindness in children is an exceptional condition. This has been realized in gathering the experimental data over five consecutive years, thus allowing new pupils to be tested each year. Consequently, independent statistical comparisons were further made with sighted groups. By contrast, in recent studies and because of the difficulties of finding CB children as subjects, there is generally one CB group whose age range is very large: 12 CB aged 5.7-to-9.6 in Cromer (1973), 15 CB aged eight-to-11 in one of Gottesman's groups (1973), 13 CB aged 9.10-to-16.10 in Davidson et al. (1981), etc. Each blind subject of these small samples is then strictly matched with a sighted one according to a set of variables. Given the high variability of the blind subjects' performances, some inconsistencies observed in the results may stem from the difference in the methods used.

The second aspect to be emphasized is that, since the various experiments reported in 1966 were conducted successively over five years, each CB child was not tested in all the Piagetian tasks studied. This precluded any analysis of intra-subject variability, and the intertask comparisons concern only the mean group performances. Intra-subject variability, as Friedman and Pasnak (1973) have studied it in two types of tasks, is of course an interesting measure. But biases due to the order of presentation may occur, and these effects are difficult to control in the blind subjects because of the small samples generally available.

Let us now examine to what extent recent empirical data affect my observations.

Extensive reviews on spatial behavior in the blind are available (Hatwell 1978, Millar 1981) and show significant differences in comparing CB and NS or BS children. For strictly Piagetian tasks, Millar (1976) found that in rotation and perspective problems, self-referent coding tendencies are more salient and persist longer in the CB than in the BS, and Stephens (1977) observed too a very marked lag in the achievement of these spatial problems by the CB.

In conservation tasks, Miller (1969) showed that at age 10, CB have not yet attained substance, weight and volume conservation, and Tobin (1972) found his CB sample to be significantly inferior to the NS. Delays in the achievement of conservation are reported too by Gottesman (1973) and by Stephens (1977) in substance, weight and volume problems. Moreover, Davidson et al. (1981) observed that, although CB children showed more sophisticated exploratory hand movements than BS ones, there was a 3.5-year-mean difference in the age at which CB and BS children reached substance conservation. Only in Cromer's research (1973) did the CB perform as well as the BS and the NS in substance conservation. Taken together, these studies on spatial and physical concepts have therefore generally confirmed my earlier observations.

Data in concrete classification tasks are less consistent. Higgins (1973) found no significant difference between CB, BS and NS groups aged five-to-11 years, although the scores of the blind were always inferior to those of the sighted. In his opinion, the impairment of the blind "was a product of deficient perceptual input and absent visual imagery rather than a reflection of a developmental lag in the attainment of classificatory logic." By contrast, Stephens (1977) showed that the CB were markedly inferior to the NS in class inclusion, intersection of classes and changing classification criterion, while their performances were as good as those of the NS in simple classification tasks. In addition, both Higgins and Stephens found that the basis on which the child has to reason has a significant effect: the same problem being correctly performed or failed according to the nature of the objects to be classified. This factor may account for the discrepancies observed in Higgins's and Stephens's results since the material they used was not the same, and is consistent with my 1966's work hypotheses. It also suggests that further work in classificatory behaviors in the blind should adopt the contemporary approach in which logic classes are distinguished from the empirical collections effected by the child in some situations (see, for example, Markman, 1978).

The only new data that are available on seriation tasks are those of Friedman and Pasnak (1973) who designed an experiment to test my 1966 assertions. Twenty-one (21) blind children aged six-to-14 were each tested against a set of classification and seriation problems. Most of these tests required that the child manipulate concrete objects, one was the verbally presented analog of a concrete oddity problem and another was the verbal analog of a concrete problem of size seriation. Unfortunately, this interesting design was applied to a highly questionable sample of blind children: only nine out of 21 subjects were congenitally blind and only 12 out of 21 were totally blind. The scores of the CB were not further separated from those of the others and, in the main statistical analysis, the scores of the totally blind were not separated from those of the partially seeing children. The data from this research cannot therefore be interpreted in terms of the questions discussed here.

It can therefore be concluded from the above review that the developmental lag of the blind evidenced in 1966 has been confirmed in further work as far as spatial representation and conservation are concerned and, to some degree, in concrete classification tasks.

It is impossible to evaluate today the pertinence of my results showing that CB are less impaired (or not impaired) in verbal logical tasks, since no attempt to replicate this part of the research was reported. Yet, it is in the area of the CB's verbal behavior that, in my opinion, some studies are needed today. In fact, two arguments suggest that language development may actually not be strictly equivalent in the CB and the NS children, as I had assumed in 1966 on the basis of informal observations. First, and due to the high variability of the blind's performances, I have used only non-parametric statistical tests. These tests are less powerful than the parametric ones, and a type II error (not rejecting the null hypothesis when it should have been rejected) may have biased the comparison of verbal operations in the blind and the sighted. Secondly, substantial progress has been made in recent developmental psycholinguistic research. In using modern psycholinguistic concepts and methods to assess the logical components of verbal behavior, the real language competence of the CB may appear to be somewhat different from that of the sighted. Fraiberg's observations (1977) on blind babies support this assumption since she has found, in addition to a marked delay in the attainment of object permanency, that language achievement was not exactly the same in CB and NS infants.

In conclusion, substantial knowledge of the cognitive development of the CB is available today, but much work is still to be done in this area. My hope is that further research will provide a better understanding of the functional significance of the differences observed between blind and sighted children and, as a result, will help to achieve efficient educational programs for the blind.

Yvette Hatwell
Grenoble, 1984

See "References" for details of all cited material.

Foreword and Introduction to the French Edition, 1966

The research presented here was done under the auspices of the Laboratory for Experimental Psychology of the Sorbonne. To Professor Paul Fraisse, who has carefully directed my research, and who has constantly guided and inspired me by his comments and his encouragement, I express my profound and sincere gratitude.

My research also owes much to Professor Jean Piaget, whose courses I had the privilege of taking while at the Sorbonne, and who paid me the great honor, some years later, of taking an interest in my work and welcoming me to the International Center of Genetic Epistemology in Geneva. I hope that he will view with approval this work, which comes out of my devotion and attachment to his principles.

The scientific approach and amicable collaboration which I found at the Laboratory for Experimental Psychology at the Sorbonne have been very precious to me. To my colleagues and friends—researchers and technicians—I address my most heartfelt thanks.

I would like finally to express my thanks to the directors and professors of the National Institute of the Young Blind, in Paris, and of the Seine Regional Institute of the Blind, at Saint-Mandé, as well as to the administrator and teachers of the primary and nursery schools of Paris, who have opened their schools to me, and given me the facilities to carry out the research presented here.

Introduction

The study of sensory deprivations and of their repercussions on the development of intelligence belongs to a generalized field of research which is concerned with the connections between "perception" and "cognition." For a long time the role conferred upon sensory perceptions within the developments of cognitive structures served both as delineator of diverse philosophies and also as a point of attack for those opposed to them. From rationalism to empiricism, we either have allotted to abstract concepts and reason a preeminence based upon the partial and deceptive perceptions of our senses, or we have considered experience, and more particularly sensory experience, basic to cognitive processes.

With the development of modern psychology, two main avenues have been used to approach the problem of the relations between perception and intelligence:

1. by studying the particular structural properties of perceptive and of intellectual mechanisms, not only were analogies brought to light, but the profound differences which characterize each of them were also revealed;

2. by studying the reciprocal functions of these mechanisms, during the acquisition of cognitive structures and during the development of high mental activities, cognitive inferences within perceptions were revealed. In certain cases it was shown that sensory perceptions help reasoning, but also noted was the possibility of "conflict" when perceptual stimuli cannot be integrated within a logical framework.

It is generally assumed that a main characteristic of intellectual processes is to allow the individual to go beyond the immediacy of perceptions. The problem is then to know to what extent these processes are dependent on perceptual knowledge. If perceived data actually need to be referred to a logical framework to become intelligible, will this framework be constructed in an autonomous way or will it depend to a certain degree on the nature of perceptive feedbacks from the external reality? These two questions are the basic theme of the work presented here.

Different methods have been used to approach the problem. Experimental and developmental genetic studies have proceeded with a systematic analysis of the perceptive and intellectual development of the child in an effort to find out how progress in one of the sectors provides feedback for another, and, in doing so, improves the structures of the latter.

Psychopathology also has contributed interesting data. Starting from the intellectual and logical deficiency which characterizes the mentally retarded, it seeks to determine how perceptive structures develop among subjects whose intellectual and cognitive limitations are known.

Starting from a perceptual deficiency of external origin, the inverse method seeks to determine how this deficiency affects intellectual operations. The study of sensory deficits utilizes the experimental paradigm. Of the two major types of sensory deprivation—deafness and blindness—the former has been the subject of most of the earlier studies. These studies show that deafness in the young child have drastic effects on language acquisition, so they are mainly concerned with the problem of the relation between language and thought. However, the symbolic and conceptual deficiency due to the absence of language which inevitably accompanies early deafness, makes it impossible to separate the specific effects that sensory deprivation, as such, has on intellectual processes. As will be demonstrated later, early blindness has more of these characteristics. A study of the psychological development of blind children makes it possible to determine how perceptual data are utilized and how they are integrated into logical reasoning. Therefore, the problem of how perceptual data are integrated and affect logical reasoning will be studied here by a systematic analysis of the cognitive development of blind children.

The purpose of this work is thus to probe the specific effects that blindness—considered as sensory deprivation—has upon the functioning of the intelligence of the child. In order to properly state the problem we must first analyze the exact nature of the handicap presented by blindness, particularly congenital blindness. Therefore, in Chapter I there is consideration of the sensory equipment which remains at the disposal of the blind child. The question will be: To what extent do the tactile perceptions—which evidently become of prime importance in blind persons—take the place of the missing visual ones? A review of the literature devoted to the philosophical as well as psychological aspects of the problem, will promote awareness of the distinctive and perhaps irreducible characteristics of visual and tactile modalities.

It will be shown that, owning to the fragmentary character of tactile perceptions, the perceptual knowledge of the blind child is much poorer than that of the sighted. Therefore, early blindness results in a "natural" impoverishment of the amount of sensory stimulations available to the child.

Literature on the blind in this area has dealt generally with the nature of tactile perceptions, and has considered whether or not the blind were able to generate the notion of space. Nevertheless, there has also been some research concerning the effects that blindness and sensory deprivations in general have on the development of the intelligence. A review of this work is proposed in Chapter I.

In Chapter II there is a statement of the problem to be investigated, the theoretical frame of reference, and the working hypothesis from which the different experiments were derived.

Such is the content of the first part of this work. The second part describes our own experiences. Finally, in a third part, we analyze the results, their significance, and their limitations.

Yvette Hatwell
Paris, 1966

Preface to the
French Edition, 1966

Did intelligence appear more complex to Aristotle than the atom to Democritus? Today, decade by decade, we have become aware of the prodigious complexity of the atom, yet we are still far from having grasped the structure of intelligence. To man intelligence seemed to be the natural power of his mind, however, he tended to consider it as an intuitive gift, and was content to admire its achievements. Only when such psychologists as Binet and Spearman tried to measure intelligence did we gradually become aware of its make-up and scope.

Even though significant results were attained, especially when factor analytic techniques were used to identify the components of intellectual activities, a clear understanding of the intelligence of the adult person occurred only when the genetic approach was used by Jean Piaget and his school. This approach allows us to witness the step-by-step development of successive intellectual modalities. Within this framework, a special place belongs to those studies based on the unfortunate conditions of Nature that deprive some children of visual or auditory perceptions from birth.

What repercussions does the deprivation of stimuli and feedback from one or more of the senses have on the development of intelligence? For a long time we have known that deafness is accompanied by muteness which limits the development of language and thereby cognitive processes. However, there have been far fewer studies on the effects of blindness on these faculties.

Yvette Hatwell's work fills this gap. With tireless patience she has continued to analyze the effect which early deprivation of visual perception has upon the development of intelligence. Her work is a contribution to the understanding of the blind and at the same time, of the laws of intelligence.

I wish to underline the links between the value of her conclusions and the quality of her methods. Starting with Piaget's conception as a frame of reference, she contributed her own experimental results. She is particularly to be commended for recognizing that a few astute observations are not sufficient proof of a theory or demonstration. Her work proves that it is possible and fruitful to test a hypothesis through properly designed experimentation. She used existing measures and devised new ones to compare the behavior of blind children with that of the sighted. This approach enabled her not only to analyze with precision the repercussions that blindness has on the development of intelligence, but also to extend our knowledge concerning the relations between perception and cognition.

From her abundant harvest of findings I have chosen to underline her documentation of the difficulty that man has in arriving at a perfect representation of spatial dimension when he can use only *successive* tactile-motor exploration to construct it. That certain something which *simultaneous* visual perception gives is always lacking in such representations. We know that the congenitally blind are not able to recognize visual forms immediately after corrective surgery. Yvette

Hatwell's work confirms the fact that the adventititously blind, who had sight during their first few years of life (even though it was at a time when they were not able to handle spatial connections), do not suffer the same deficiencies as the congenitally blind. Eyesight is truly the sense which perceives simultaneity; successiveness can only give a figurative approximation of it. Among blind children this deficiency slows down the development of the operations leading to the conceptualization of the permanence of the object and the establishments of a network of reciprocal relations between objects.

In striking opposition, as soon as logical operations, which deal only with concepts, are freed from their perceptive contingencies, the blind find themselves on an equal footing with the sighted. Can it be that within intelligence, the development of figurative and symbolic structures is governed by different sets of laws? We need wonder no more since the present work provides precise answers with astonishing clarity and insight.

Paul Fraisse
Paris, 1966

Editor's Preface to the English Edition, 1984

When effort is made to address the educational needs of persons with various types of handicaps there is swift realization that in order to program effectively one must first know the patterning of cognitive abilities and deficits that these persons bring to the learning situation. Piaget, the Swiss psychologist, supplied us with the milestones that chart the course of cognitive development from infancy to adulthood. He and members of his Geneva group also furnished a battery of assessments that measured the ability to reason concretely and abstractly. As Barbel Inhelder (1968) devised or adapted portions of this assessment battery to achieve *A Diagnosis of Reasoning in the Mentally Retarded* (1968), she supplied the first application of the theory to an analysis of cognitive development in exceptional persons. Thus, the usefulness of the approach was documented. Yvette Hatwell's *Sensory Deprivation and Intelligence* (published in French in 1966) is the first major effort to use Piagetian reasoning assessments to analyze cognitive development, or more specifically, the operational thought processes, of blind persons. Her study supplies a detailed analysis of observed inconsistencies in the cognitive processes of blind children and youth, and through application of Piagetian theory she traces these inconsistencies back to their inception in infancy and early childhood.

In her writing Hatwell supplies the reader with an excellent overview of eighteenth century philosophical opinion on the contribution of visual and tactual cues in the establishment of concepts. As she traces the enlargements of knowledge concerning perception and cognition in blind persons over the past two centuries, a detailed analysis also is provided of the disparities existing in theories dealing with the conception of space and blindness as effort was made to determine if spatial properties which accompany tactual perceptions have an optical origin.

With penetrating insight that evolves from a thorough grounding in Piagetian theory and from work with blind persons, Hatwell emphasizes the distinction between the *figurative* and *operative* aspects of cognitive functions. The figurative aspect characterizes forms of cognition which appear to a person as "copies of reality"; the three fundamental varieties of figurative knowledge are: (1) perception (i.e., actual perception of an object); (2) imitation (gesture, sound, drawing, etc.); and (3) mental images (i.e., internalized reproduction of an object) (Gruber, 1977). The *operative* aspect refers to the action aspect of intelligence and is the fundamental aspect of knowledge that "operates on a reality state"; that is, "it is the essential, generalizable structuring aspect of intelligence insofar as knowing means constructing, transforming, incorporating, etc." (Furth, 1969, pp. 135, 263).

In Piagetian theory, figurative structures play a supportive role in cognition, i.e., they furnish the symbolic materials (mental images, etc.) utilized in cognitive operations. Because blindness entails damage to the figurative structures, i.e., decreases in perceptions and their figurative representations, Hatwell saw need to determine if a diminution of perceptual knowledge would have a detrimental effect on intellectual processes. To do this she compared the performance of congenitally blind (blind at birth or during the first year of life) with adventitiously blind (blind after the age of four) and sighted children who were matched on IQ (i.e., Verbal IQ was 80 or above) on reasoning assessments which involved *logic = mathematical operations* (operations which establish relations between given objects, e.g. classification, seriation, numbers, similarities and differences) and reasoning assessments which involved *infralogical operations* (operations which involved a representative imagery and which promote consideration of such spatial relationships as space and time, proximity and separation).

Since blindness imposes limitations on a person's perception of the surrounding world and the representative images of it, greater deficits would be expected in spatial and physical infralogical operations which center on the object itself or on a representative image than in logical operations, operations which center on relations between objects. Hatwell's findings confirm these expectations and also supply evidence that blind persons perform more successfully on purely verbal tests than on tests of equivalent logical structures which involve concrete objects.

In her study, the performance of congenitally blind subjects on assessments designed to measure spatial infralogical operations was inferior to that of the adventitiously blind subjects, and when the congenitally blind group was compared with the sighted group, delays of four-to-six years were found. However, when comparison involved only older subjects, it was noted that at later ages the congenitally blind subjects did achieve concepts of space similar to those of the sighted subjects. Thus, Hatwell suggests that visual deprivation delays rather than precludes spatial representation.

On assessments which measure physical infralogical operation (realization that the amount, weight and volume of two identical balls of clay remain the same even though one of the balls is transformed into the shape of a sausage) the performance of the congenitally blind subjects, when compared with that of the sighted subjects, reflected delays of two-to-three years. The serendipitous finding was that understanding of the invariance of weight was more delayed in the congenitally blind subjects than was the delay in understanding of the amount or substance.

On classification tasks that dealt with perceptual contrasts and involved logical operations the performance of the congenitally blind subjects was significantly lower than that of the adventitiously blind subjects. When compared with sighted subjects, delays evidenced by the congenitally blind subjects were as great as three-to-four years. Additionally, when compared with the sighted subjects, the congenitally blind subjects had average delays of two years on tasks which required classification of geometric forms and changing criterion, and delays of one to three years on seriation tasks. But on verbal tasks involving logical situations the performance of the congenitally blind subjects was either superior, equivalent or approximate to that of the sighted subjects.

As she utilized Piagetian theory in the interpretation of her findings, Hatwell posited that the blind experienced a "rupture of equilibrium" between assimilation and accommodation). Loss of sight was accompanied by a decrease in the pressure from the outside world, i.e. the blind person cannot and does not attend to visual perceptions, thus the demand and the capacity to accommodate to outside reality is impaired, but the assimilatory potentials do not have an equivalent deficiency. The blind person may have the instruments of thought required to integrate incoming data into existing cognitive structures, but blindness has limited the acquisition and control of his inputs. As a result his generalizations may be maladaptive or inaccurate. The figurative aspects of cognition, "copies of reality," are impaired by blindness and "intense repercussions" result.

The importance of infant intervention programs is underscored by the finding that congenitally blind subjects exhibited performance that was significantly inferior to the performance of the adventitiously blind subjects in situations involving purely verbal reasoning versus their inadequacy in reasoning situations that required the manipulation of concrete objects underscores the need to involve these persons in activities that require ongoing interaction with objects.

Thus, Hatwell has furnished documentation of delays in the development of reasoning in congenitally blind children, delays which have been the subject of philosophical speculations for more than two centuries. Her study provides the first step in programming for exceptional persons, identification and analysis of deficits. Following this, efforts are indicated which provide intervention programs aimed at remediation and prevention. As these two subsequent steps are achieved it will be remembered that Yvette Hatwell instigated the analytical cognitive mapping required for their accomplishment.

Beth Stephens
Washington, D.C., 1984

Part One

HISTORY AND STATEMENT OF THE PROBLEM

Chapter One

REVIEW OF THE LITERATURE

Comparison of Visual and Tactual Sensory Modalities

From the epistemological viewpoint, the main difference between eyesight and touch lies in the close proximity between subject and object required for actual tactual perception. Because of this "direct contact" requirement, the tactual perceptive field is more limited than the visual one. Tactual exploration partially compensates for this limitation since it makes possible the perception of a whole object (provided it is of manageable size). Yet tactual perception remains fragmentary because it proceeds gradually, part by part, in the exploration of the total object, and a final synthesis is necessary to reconstruct the entire object from the successive perceptions of its components.

Historically, a great number of studies have concentrated on the relationship between visual and tactual perceptions. They have employed two distinct approaches: in one, studies were made of the congenitally blind immediately after sight was made possible through surgical intervention; in the other, there was comparison of tactual performances of the congenitally blind who had not been operated on with those of the temporary blind: i.e., normally sighted, but blindfolded, individuals.

Therefore we shall examine step-by-step the information on these two approaches provided by works of a literary and psychological nature.

Sight Restoration in Congenitally Blind Persons

Consideration is given the initial question formulated by Molyneux, as well as the studies it gave rise to and which influenced the philosophy and psychology of the 18th and 19th centuries; then review is made of contributions of animal experimentations and the recent advancements of ophthalmological surgery. This should then enable us to tell what psychology may expect from the data on the gaining of sight by blind animals and human beings.

Molyneux's question and related studies

In 1690, John Locke, in *An Essay Concerning Human Understanding,* noted the question which his friend, W. Molyneux of Dublin, persistently asked:

"Suppose a man born blind, and now adult, and taught by touch to distinguish between a cube and a sphere of the same metal, and of the same size, so as to tell which is the cube, and which is the sphere, when he felt one and then the other. Suppose then the cube and sphere are placed on a table, and the blind man made to see; *quaere,* By using his sight, before touching them, could he now distinguish and tell which is the cube, which the sphere? To which the acute and judicious professor answers: 'No. For though he has obtained the experience of how a cube, how a sphere, affects his touch, he has not yet realized that which affects his touch must affect his sight, or that a protruberant angle in the cube, that pressing his hand unequally, will appear to his eye as the cube.'"

Locke had no difficulty in accepting Molyneux's viewpoint ("I agree with this thinking gentleman, whom I am proud to call my friend"); actually, the statement supported Locke's general theory, since it implied that there is no direct, purely intellectual correlation between the perceptions of our different senses other than the ones empirically learned. But because the blind man who later gains sight cannot visually distinguish a sphere from a cube at the first attempt, it cannot be assumed, as it was done later, that the blind are deprived of spatial concepts. For Locke, space is a "simple idea" and the blind reach it from their tactual perceptions just as well as the sighted. What is missing to the blind is the connection between the tactual clues they have learned to use and the visual ones which are new to them when vision is gained or restored. As Warnock notes, in the appendix to the 1960 work by von Senden, Locke's blind man is unaware only of the visual appearance of things; therefore, there is implicit admission that visual appearance is not the essential aspect of spatial perception.

For his part, Leibniz (1704) went much further. For him, geometric space was a form of abstraction which did not need visual imagery: the concept of space remained essentially the same for the congenitally blind, who arrived at it purely from tactual perceptions, as for the totally paralytic who perceived only visually. Both of them would arrive at the same geometrical concept since its elaboration would call only for abstract connections.

After lengthy observation of the blind man of Le Puiseaux, Diderot, in his *Lettre sur les aveugles* (1749), was obviously impressed by the high degree of precision and skill with which he used tactual perceptual cues. Consequently, he rejected the hypothesis that the blind were deprived of spatial concepts; his position was reinforced by the example of Saunderson, the famous blind geometrician. Adopting a viewpoint similar to Leibniz's, Diderot, in his *Lettre sur les sourds et muets,* attempted to imagine what life would be like if individuals who have the use of only one sense each (either vision, or touch or smell, etc.) lived together as a group. He hypothesizes that they would consider each other to be insane, but that they would get along beautifully as far as geometry, but *only* geometry, is concerned.

A quite different view of the same question was taken by Berkeley in 1709. While he agreed with Molyneux and Locke on basic facts, his interpretation of them was entirely different. For him, eyesight and touch were opposite modalities, and only touch, which calls for a direct contact with the objects would lead to the notion of space. Except for the interpretation of light and colors, eyesight could convey only "the deceitful appearance of things," vision, in itself, carried no spatial cue, and it would be only through simple, inductive connections that certain spatial tactual cues would be linked to visual perceptions. If Molyneux's blind man could not recognize the sphere, it was because he had not yet been able to establish the connection between spatial concepts of tactual origin and corresponding visual cues. In other words, the blind are deprived only of the appearance of things, not of spatial concepts, which are strictly tactual in origin.

In London, in 1728, Cheselden performed a successful operation on a young congenitally blind boy, and recorded his observations on the patient's post-operative reactions. The young boy declared that "things were touching his eyes," a comment which was frequently quoted, but which, because of its vagueness, was given various interpretations. Moreover, in his report to the Royal Society in London, Cheselden says that the boy did not recognize the shape of anything, and did not distinguish one object from another even when they were of different shape and size (von Senden, 1932).

It can be seen that Cheselden's observations tended to confirm Molyneux's prediction: the first visual impressions were effectively meaningless for those who achieved sight via surgery. However, in terms of their theoretical and philosophical implications they could confirm Locke's ideas as well as Berkeley's. As a matter of fact, the lack of experimental control (Revesz, 1950; Wertheimer, 1951) in the performance of Cheselden's operation, as well as in many others which followed, did not permit conclusive statements, a point which will be reconsidered.

Let us return to the different philosophical theories concerning space and blindness. In diametric opposition to Berkeley, Platner, in 1785, after having observed a blind subject for several weeks, stated that sight alone, being the domain of simultaneity, could lead to the notion of space. Tactual perception, which proceeds by successive steps, is temporally distributed and could not have a spatial tenor. Platner held that the blind substituted time for space: i.e., the tactual impressions the blind receive are distributed within temporal intervals. He warned, however, that the verbal practices of the blind frequently were deceitful and tended to promote illusions concerning their real ability in constructing tactual space. This theory, which was as extreme as Berkeley's, aroused many reactions. During the first part of the 20th century, workers tried either to demonstrate its excessive and unacceptable character or to confirm it through experimentation tenor. Platner held that the blind substituted time for space: i.e., the tactual impressions the blind receive are distributed within temporal intervals. He warned, however, that the verbal practices of the blind frequently were deceitful and tended to promote illusions concerning their real ability in constructing tactual space. This theory, which was as extreme as Berkeley's, aroused many reactions. During the first part of the 20th century, workers tried either to demonstrate its excessive and unacceptable character or to confirm it through experimentation.

Steinberg (1920) observed and questioned ten blind adults, and, as a result, he found it impossible to accept Platner's ideas: i.e., to deny that the blind achieved a certain notion of space. He preferred the distinction, which was introduced by Heller in 1895, between (1) near space, which can be embraced by only one hand or by both hands close together (the only method totally available to the blind), and (2) extended space, which can be explored by using both arms but which is difficult to comprehend without the use of sight, and finally (3) still more extended space, which calls for a displacement of the body and therefore is not employed by the blind. Such an interpretation was discussed by Villey (1930) as he reviewed his own experiences in questioning several blind adults. He noted individual differences in the ability to arrive at "spatial synthetic representations" from tactual perceptions. He did affirm, however, that the blind man was perfectly capable of arriving at the construction of a total spatial object by liberating himself from the impressions peculiar to tactual scanning and the limitations inherent in its fragmentary and successive character.

Continuing in Platner's steps, Hagen (1844) held that touch does not allow for spatial discrimination: "The ability to feel, in itself, never informs one of the exact location of the stimulus; this information can be arrived at only through correlated visual impressions which are learned through continued practice. The representations of position is not a matter of touch, any more than that of extension or shape. When two points are touched on my skin, I do not feel any information concerning how far apart they are. First I must locate them visually, and then measure the distance between them while my imagination engulfs my entire body. Such is the process for all estimations of tactual dimensions" (Delay, 1935, p. 244).

Gelb and Goldstein (1920) have reported a clinical observation supporting Platner's and Hagen's conception: following an occipital cerebral lesion, a young man manifested trouble in tactual perception of forms and in stereognosia, in addition to the visual defects usually observed in these cases. They concluded that tactual perception has no spatial characteristics, and that the only existing space is visual.

Although their observations in this instance have great value in the understanding of certain relations between vision and touch Gelb and Goldstein arrive at conclusions that are not fully supported by their experimental findings. Indeed, as Delay (1935) emphasizes, only if the loss of tactual representation *always* follows the loss of visual representations can we accept such conclusions, and these conclusions have not been confirmed by psychopathology. After losing his visual representations and, subsequently, his tactual ones, the patient also would have to be able to work out a new type of tactually-represented space; this incapacity has not been demonstrated. Similar considerations lead Ajuriaguerra and Hecaen (1960) to object to such generalizations from a rare and exceptional case.

In his work *Space and Sight,* von Senden (1932) arrived at conclusions which tend to concur with those of Platner and Hagen. Starting with the "Cheselden case," Von Senden reviewed all the research which dealt with the spatial conception of the congenitally blind after their establishment of sight through surgical intervention. After issuing a warning about the fragile nature of observations obtained mainly from minimally controlled experiments, von Senden successively reviewed the remarks of subjects, before and after their operations, concerning their perception of shapes, distances, volumes, etc. From his review there is indication that first post-operative visual impressions are rarely meaningful to the previously blind subjects; attaching verbal labels to visually presented objects is impossible, as is the attribution of meaning to these objects, even the most familiar ones. On the other hand, there is indication that for certain subjects a differentiation of shapes is possible; these subjects affirm seeing two or more objects, but are incapable of naming them, describing them (large, small, etc.), or counting them.

Von Senden interprets these facts as clearly showing that "the congenitally blind do not have, *a priori,* a concept of space; they do not acquire it from the localization of sensations on their skin, nor from the kinesthetic sensations associated with the movement of their limbs. Verbal concepts partly replace the deficiency of the perceptions. These temporal schemata. . . have nothing spatial about them. The space concepts (of the blind) are therefore intellectual achievements only, without any sensory basis; they cannot be more than a surrogate for the spatial awareness he lacks" (1960, pp. 289–290). Von Senden's position approximates Platner's; he, too, finds no reason to accept the notion of "tactile space."

Hebb's interest in the results of von Senden's work is well-documented and will be discussed later along with the use he made of them. Indeed, it is proper to distinguish on one hand, the essential documentary contribution of von Senden's study and on the other the interpretations he, as author, makes of these observations. These studies serve to establish the need for post-operative visual perceptive training, training which often is long, laborious, and possibly even disappointing to the patient. Need for the training recently was confirmed in a paper by Pokrovskii. Unfortunately, we only know about this paper from a brief critique by I. London (1960). As Director of the Voronezh Ophthalmologic Clinic and Medical Institute, Pokrovskii performed operations on two congenitally blind boys (one 10 years old and the other of unknown age) and made the following observations:

1. Both boys were incapable of immediate recognition of visually perceived objects; their common reaction was: "I can see something, but I don't know what";

2. Visual differentiation of the shape of the objects was impossible, as was differentiation of size or volume;

3. Visual perception of the distance and the number of the objects also was inaccurate;

4. Tactually, all these aspects were perfectly perceived.

Progress, although slow, was recorded during the post-operation period of observation. Pokrovskii discussed these cases, as well as others concerned with the restoration of vision in blind adults, in terms of the Pavlovian theory of sensory analysis.

So, although variable, research findings generally agree on the behavior of the blind who gain their vision. In interpreting the findings, however, von Senden adopted a position as dogmatic as Platner's or Berkeley's, and *neglected to specify the criteria on which he based the existence or non-existence* of the "spatial concepts" of which he spoke. Indeed, it is not clearly understood how difficulties in the utilization of visual perceptions, as encountered by the formerly blind but subsequently surgically sighted, are proof of the non-existence of a tactile space. It seems to us, rather, to emphasize the importance of the progressive perceptual training through which an individual proceeds, from birth onward, as well as the essential role of experience in the coordination of the different sensory functions (Revesz, 1950). As for "tactual space," it seems essential first to define the characteristic behaviors corresponding to the possession or the non-possession of spatial concepts, and then determine which behaviors belong to the congenitally blind prior to surgical intervention.

Before considering the contributions deriving from animal experimentation, Revesz's position (1950) will be reviewed. From his strict phenomenological viewpoint (i.e., the level of immediate impression), the visual world, the tactile world, and the auditory or olfactory worlds, have nothing in common. If, practically, there is a correlation between visual and "haptic"—tactilo-kinesthetic—perceptions, it is because both of them deal with the "spatial nature" of exterior objects, and this correlation is progressively established. This is why Revesz does not accept the conclusions that von Senden derives from the difficulties which the congenitally blind encounter in post-operative visual discriminations. Although he posits that haptic perception is autonomous and governed by specific laws which do not necessarily apply to visual perception, Revesz conceded to the congenitally blind a certain conception of space, a conception which may be quite different from that of the sighted, but which it seems to him illegitimate to deny.

We now turn to the chief results obtained from animal experimentation, results which will lead us to make several reservations on the interpretation of data obtained after sight is surgically provided to the congenitally blind.

Findings from animal studies

Early work by Riesen (1947) generated experimental research on the effects of sensory deprivation among animals. The first studies on the behavior of chimpanzees raised in darkness during the first months of their lives were carried on by Hebb (1949), who, on the basis of these and of von Senden's findings, emphasized the importance of early training in the establishment of perceptive structures. The emphasis placed on the variety and the extent of sensory stimulations during infancy engendered a flow of studies that was of considerable volume.

Riesen (1947) raised chimpanzees in darkness, either total or partial, until they were seven or eight months old in order to study their level of visual discrimination. He established a systematic and generally irreversible inferiority of these subjects in comparison with individuals raised in a situation of normal visual stimulation. Hebb's studies (1949) with rats took the same course. From these studies, Hebb inferred that visual "Gestalts" are not inborn, but instead are formed during the first months of life, and deprivation of visual stimulation during this period can impair their subsequent establishment.

In an effort to disprove Molyneux's hypothesis, Nissen, Chow, and Semmes (1951) raised a chimpanzee under conditions that deprived it as far as possible of tactual and kinesthetic stimulation. In order to limit tactual stimulation and motor activity, they fastened cardboard cylinders to the four limbs of the animal. When the protective cylinders were removed a few months later, they observed important disorders in psychomotor coordination, raising of the threshold of discrimination between two points and of the integration of tactilo-kinesthetic perceptions.

However, Riesen pointed out that the lack of visual stimulation during early infancy also affects the *structure* of receptors and optical nerve paths, and that these effects are irreversible if the deprivation is prolonged. Similar results were obtained by Brattgard (1952) and by Siegel (1953).

The harm done to tissues due to non-use of receptors is of practical as well as theoretical interest because it suggests the need for stimulation of sensory organs if they are to remain organically sound. Moreover, these facts serve to question Hebb's utilization of Riesen's results. The visual discriminatory difficulties encountered by the chimpanzees as they slowly regain the use of their sight may very well be related to the deterioration of certain structures of the eye, the nerve paths, or the optical cortical projections.

Recent contributions from ophthalmology and ophthalmological surgery

Major implications derive from operations for the removal of congenital cataract, from functional re-education of persons who have strabismus in any of its forms, and from the education of amblyopic children.

1. *Operations for congenital cataract.* If it were possible to repeat Cheselden's experiment under scientifically controlled conditions, would it resolve unanswered questions? If the criteria of contemporary ophthalmologists were applied they would impose reservations on the interpretation of these earlier "recoveries" of the congenitally blind.

Molyneux's supposition that an adult can suddenly regain sight is difficult to conceive today. Indeed, operations for congenital cataract must be performed in early childhood, around the sixth month according to some, or between the second and fourth years according to others (Bouzas, 1955). After that age, any functional recovery is gravely endangered. Therefore, cases similar to the ones mentioned by Pokrovskii can occur only in backward areas where visually impaired persons are not given early and systematic medical attention. These operations are performed in several stages, and the progressive recovery takes months, or sometimes years, further more, the operation is never completely successful—i.e., the visual acuity of the individual is rarely more than 40 percent of that of the average person. In other words, his visual acuity, following surgical intervention, is that of an *amblyopic* eye.

Often, the limited visual recovery is due in part to the existence of other malformations which affect various ocular organs and which frequently serve to complicate the congenital cataract condition. The phenomenon of nystagmus which generally occurs after surgical intervention on the crystalline lens also must be noted. This phenomenon, which can be either transitory or permanent, greatly inconveniences the patient during the initial recovery period. Similarly, because sudden brightness can incite very painful contractions, post-operative luminous stimulations must be progressively introduced and strictly controlled.

Because of the findings of Riesen, Siegel, and others, secondary injuries due to the lack of sensory stimulations during the first months or the first years of infancy must be listed along with other limiting factors. Progressive and irreversible deterioration of certain tissues, which impairs the chances of a substantial sight recovery, serves to complicate congenital malformations. Studies concerned with cross-eyed and amblyopic children provide interesting data in this area.

2. *Functional re-education of the strabismic and schooling of amblyopic children:* Because the retinal image transmitted from a strabismic eye is inhibited at the cortical level, visual perception tends to be monocular. Surgical intervention which rectifies strabismus must be followed by orthopedic exercises which are designed to reestablish binocular vision. There is note, however, that while disuse impairs the visual acuity of the affected eye prior to the operation, post-operative exercises can be effective only if the operation is performed early in youth—i.e., prior to ages seven or eight. After that age, the ambylopia of the weaker eye and insufficiency of binocular vision both tend to limit vision. As noted by Riesen, visual acuity depends in part on the use of receptors.

Similar problems are raised by the visually impaired or true amblyopic persons. Although their limited vision distinguishes them from blind persons, these children experience difficulty in functioning in standard academic situations. When they become proficient in the use of Braille they make limited use of their residual vision, and usually a decline in visual acuity can be seen in conjunction with this non-use of the receptors. Verification of such impairment is provided by Delthil.*

The conclusion which emanates from these observations is that the earlier accounts of operations which restored sight to blind adults must be interpreted with caution. It seems unlikely that we shall see Cheselden's experiment repeated under carefully controlled conditions. Although accounts of surgically treated congenitally blind persons were strongly present in the philosophical and psychological literature of the 18th and 19th centuries, it now seems appropriate to question their validity as a basis for statements concerning the nature of tactual space.

---

*Opthalmologist at the Institut National des Jeunes Aveugles in Paris, France.

Experimental Studies on the Tactual Perception of the Blind and the Sighted

Less spectacular, perhaps, but somewhat more realistic studies in experimental psychology have taken a different approach to the problem of tactual perception. Disregarding questions on the meaning assigned to visual perceptions by the surgically treated congenitally blind, they moved toward the systematic study of the behavior of the non-treated and non-operable congenitally blind in situations which either required subtle sensory discriminations or involved the use of spatial relations.

The comparison of their performances with the performances of the sighted provides data on the nature of the organization of tactual perceptions and serves to substantiate the theory of sensory compensation. Comparison of the tactual performances of the blind with the visual performances of the sighted emphasize the differences in the "effectiveness" and the "efficiency" of each perceptual mode.

The mechanisms of tactual perception and the problem of sensory compensations

Consideration is now addressed to the basic mechanisms of tactual perception and to the tactual perception of forms and spatial relations.

1. Study of the *thresholds of tactual discrimination* among the blind and the sighted is directly related to the theory of sensory compensation ("vicariousness of the senses") discussed by Diderot (1749): "By helping each other, one sense prevents another from reaching maximum acuteness" (*Lettre sur les aveugles*). A frequent question is: "Does blindness bring about a drop in the tactual threshold? Experimental results in this field are frequently contradictory, due to lack of sufficient controls—e.g., age of subjects, age at which blindness occurred, intellectual and socio-cultural level. Kunz (1908) cites Griesbach's experiment (1899) in which the sighted are on the whole superior to the blind. On the other hand, Seashore and Ling (1918) have not found any significant difference between the two groups. Lack of difference also was noted in Plata's study (1941). On the other hand, Brown and Stratton found (1925) the blind to be significantly superior to the sighted, but in considering their results their special experimental technique must also be considered. The experimenters rejected use of the traditional esthesiometer because it was believed to neglect the active aspect in tactual perception; instead, they instructed the subjects to engage the pad of the forefinger in a sweeping motion as they touched and attempted to discriminate two fixed points on a small board. Since the motion is analogous to the one used in reading Braille the superior performance of the blind was not surprising.

A tactual experiment by Axelrod (1959) resulted in no difference between the blind and the sighted subjects. Today it is generally recognized that the threshold of tactual discrimination is not lowered in the blind, and that, in fact, the blind and the sighted are not significantly different as far as this ability is concerned. There is the suggestion, however, that the blind do profit from daily exercises which involve high level integration of more complex perceptual observations.

2. The study of tactual *geometrical illusions* is of twofold interest: first, if the same illusions are found at the tactual level as at the visual, the explanatory hypotheses such as those based on the structure of retinal receptors can be rejected; secondly, it may furnish data on the characteristics of tactual perceptive mechanisms as compared with visual ones.

Results, however, are ambiguous. Revesz (1934) found correspondence between nearly all tactual and visual geometric illusions; however, his reports gave very few details on his experimental technique, on the number and age of his subjects, and on the quantitative analysis of observed deformations. Geometrical illusions also have been described by Bean (1938). When Hatwell (1960) considered this problem she asked if the limited perceptual field and the tip of the finger analysis could alter or modify the intensity of deformations caused by field effects. Results obtained from blind subjects, age eight to 10, show that certain spatial illusions (Muller–Lyer and vertical-horizontal) do exist for the blind, but quantitatively they are less pronounced than the illusions which involve visual perception. Because of the fragmentary character of tactual perceptions other illusions (Delboeuf and Halteres) do not manifest themselves.

The tactual perception of forms and the conception of spatial relations

Spatial relations have been studied in three principal types of experimentation: mazes, matching of shapes (multiple choice, form completion, etc.), and construction of forms (writing, peg boards, and jig-saw puzzles).

1. Various experiments with *mazes* provide contradictory results. While Carr (1921) and Koch and Ufkess (1926) found the blind performed less well, Knott and Miles (1929) found the performance of the blind to be superior to that of the sighted. A lack of any differences between the two groups was reported by Duncan (1934). Because these were not well controlled experiments (some of the "blind" had partial vision), reliance could not be placed on the findings. In a more recent experiment by McFarland (1952), which was properly controlled, a superiority of the sighted over the blind was noted. Hayes (1951) questioned the appropriateness of using mazes with the blind, particularly when the results serve as an indication of the intelligence of the subjects.

2. A superiority of the sighted over the blind in a form completion task was observed by Sylvester (1913). But in the *recognition of forms* differences between blind and sighted were not clear-cut. Hayes (1933) and Worchel (1951) were not able to find significant difference between the groups. Using very complex geometrical forms Plata (1942) found a marked superiority of the blind over the sighted. Critchley (1953) held that some blind subjects have much greater ability than do the sighted. When Hatwell (1959) tested the tactual recognition of forms by children, ages eight to 16, there were no significant differences between the performances of blind and sighted of equivalent age. Similar results were reported by Ewart and Carp (1963) who concluded that visual imagery was not necessary for the recognition of forms.

To accept as conclusive the evidence obtained from one experiment on form recognition by subjects ages eight to 16 seemed questionable. The level of complexity of the forms used and the ages of the subjects must both be considered. If older children and adults are subjects, differences probably will exist only if very complex forms are used. By contrast, studies are lacking which deal with early stages of development and which employ very simple forms. It is true that the examination of blind children aged three to six or seven years is impractical, particularly if certain manipulations of objects are involved. Therefore, if no significant difference in form recognition has been observed between the blind and the sighted it may be because the phenomenon under study has become less clearly defined by age seven, a time when experimentation becomes technically feasible.

3. Very different results are obtained from studies on the *reproduction of forms* or on reconstruction of forms from separately perceived components, although each study emphasizes the difficulties encountered by the blind. The indisputable superiority of the sighted, working blindfolded, noted by Worchel (1951) can be explained by the contribution of visual imagery or visualization in tactual spatial representation. Confirmation of Worchel's results was reported by Drever (1955); in both studies the tasks included: (a) completion of a two-part form, followed by addition of two original designs to the form; and (b) by an orientation task (reconstruction of a peg on a small board after 180° of rotations of the model form); and (c) a classification task (identifying one of a series of forms which did not match the others). In 1948 Plata had observed, particularly among children ages eight to 14, an inferiority of the blind in remembering the successive positions of a point in space. Our own research (1959; 1960b) on the reproduction of geometric structures by the blind offers confirming evidence. Hunter's recent works (1964) also confirms the superiority of the sighted over the congenitally blind when the use of spatial relations is involved.

4. The difficulties encountered by the blind in activities involving spatial relations is confirmed by a *comparative study of the congenitally blind* vs. *the adventitiously blind*. Here again results point to a systematic and significant inferiority of the congenitally blind (Worchel, 1951; Drever, 1955; Hatwell, 1959). These results are contrary to the theory of compensation, since the blind prove to be either equal, or markedly inferior, to the sighted in one area, that of tactual perception, where they benefit from practice of a special kind.

When the tactual perceptions of the blind are compared with the visual perceptions of the sighted, in order to determine if the two channels are equivalent in the quantity and quality of the information they convey to the individual, the results leave no doubt about the direction and magnitude of the observed differences. The results are the same as those reported in experiments involving the reproduction of geometric designs conducted by the writer (1959); performance of a group of blind adolescents, ages 12 to 14 years, was slightly inferior to the visual performance of a sighted group which was seven years of age.

Concept of Sensory Compensation and the Nature of Tactual Space

Presently there is effort to clarify the two problems raised by the comparison of tactual performances of the blind and the sighted, namely the concept of sensory compensation and the nature of tactual space.

1. *Sensory "vicariousness."* At the level of acute sensory discrimination, the deprivation of sight does not lower the threshold of tactual acuity.

2. *Tactual space of the blind.* Philosophers of the 18th and 19th centuries questioned the existence of a purely tactual space. Did the experimental studies cited above provide partial answers?

Traditional studies concerned with the representations of space have involved the reproduction of geometrical forms, a method which considerably limited the problem. It was found, however, that performance of the congenitally blind was inferior to that of the blindfolded sighted and of the adventitiously blind and the superiority of the sighted and adventitiously blind suggested that eyesight *adds* to the tactilo-kinesthetic perception. Actually the purely tactual space of the congenitally blind, a space not extended by visual representations, is much more difficult to organize than the visual-tactual space of the sighted.

It is important to note, however, that tasks used in the study of spatial relations also required a certain motor ability in the execution of the task, thus introducing a factor that could not be controlled. By adequate experimental design and appropriate instructions we attempted to control this factor in our present experiments and isolated the representation of spatial relations as a dependent variable.

Today it would be absurd indeed to pretend that the orgin of the notion of space is exclusively either visual or tactual. Findings of genetic psychology are clear; tactilo-kinesthetic impressions are predominent during the first few weeks of life, and form the link between the organism and its environment (Wallon, 1949; Piaget, 1947). But as early as the fourth or fifth month, the coordination of sight and prehension allows the progressive fusion of tactual and proprioceptive space with visual space. After this, sight rapidly takes the lead in organizing perceptive awareness, but it is apparent that the corresponding tactilo-kinesthetic impressions continue to help structure the information conveyed through the visual channel. Sensory-motor space, perceptive space, and representative space are formed from the totality of sensory impressions.

This does not mean that representative space is a carbon copy of perceptive space nor that it is provided entirely by perceptions. Piaget has demonstrated this (Piaget–Inhelder, 1947). Obviously it is impossible to summarize in a few lines a theory as comprehensive as his; we shall cover it subsequently. Let us simply say that Piaget posits that mental space is a construction which progresses by genetic stages and it is not a simple prolongation of perception. It is the coordination of actions which lead to objective space, and this coordination is by nature intellectual and logical; the elaboration of spatial representation depends more on cognitive processes than on purely perceptive ones.

Given these conditions, the question is to find out how the perceptions (auditory, visual, and tactual for the sighted; auditory and tactual only for the blind) are used by the child in his construction of the concept of space. In this light the study of the congenitally blind takes on a renewed interest. Does the reduction of perception due to blindness create difficulties in the abstract—or "intellectual"—representation of space? The experimental studies described above do not furnish an answer when the question is put in this form. Indeed, the perceptive, motor, and cognitive aspects are so interrelated that it is impossible to determine what portion of the lowered performance of the blind is due to perceptive-motor insufficiency, and what portion is due to *insufficiencies in the logical coordination of perceptions*.

Modern theories of space, it seems, must involve both perceptive and cognitive processes. Up to now we have tried to pinpoint the knowledge that comparative studies of the blind and the sighted have contributed to the particular properties of the visual and tactual sensory modalities. Review of the psychological literature should furnish information on the relation between blindness and intelligence or, more generally, on the effect which temporary or long-term sensory deficiencies have on cognitive performances.

Effect of Sensory Deprivation on Cognitive Processes

Work by Hebb on the importance of early training and on the influence of the environment during the first few months of life has generated a wide stream of research. First, we shall examine the contributions of animal experimentation, of human experimentation, and finally by works concerned with "natural experimentation" which is the study of the sensory deficiencies.

Animal Studies

Many animal studies have been undertaken in an effort to determine the respective roles of learning and maturation in the development of differentiated behaviors. Considerable impetus has been provided by Hebb's theory. Using the *Hebb–William Intelligence Test* for rats, Hebb (1937) demonstrated that the performance of a group of rats enucleated at birth was inferior to that of a group of rats enucleated at maturity. Similarly, a group of sighted rats raised in a highly stimulating environment was found to be significantly superior to a group of equally sighted rats who were raised in the usual laboratory cages (Hebb, 1949). These results confirmed findings which evolved from Riesen's work with chimpanzees (1947), which we mentioned earlier. The effects of early deprivation were demonstrated by Hymovitch (1952) to be more pronounced than those of late deprivation; in fact, he stated that early restrictions were relatively permanent and probably irreversible (quoted by Axelrod, 1959).

Confirmation of these findings was furnished in research by Forgays and Forgays (1952), Forgus (1954), and Thompson and Heron (1954); each study notes subjects raised under conditions of sensory deprivation during their infancy exhibited systematic defeciency in problem-solving.

Human Studies

Human experiments involving sensory or environmental deprivation present obvious technical and ethical difficulties. Studies however have been conducted by Freedman, Grunebaum and Greenblatt (1961) and Vernon and McGill (1961) in- which volunteer subjects were locked up, for periods of time varying from a few hours to six or eight days, in isolated cabins in which the perceptive stimulation or the sensory-motor activity of the subjects was carefully controlled. Freedman and his colleagues (1961), Vernon, McGill and their colleagues (1961) noted that comparison of test scores obtained before and after the perceptive isolation revealed disorders in perceptive discrimination, in motor coordination, and in certain intellectual processes, the appearance of hallucinatory phenomena. However, interpretation of such experiments poses problems because it is not possible to dissociate the specific effects of sensory restrictions from an almost total restriction of motor activity (subjects were told to lie down, to engage in a minimum of body movements, and to try to "think of nothing"). A more acceptable research design was provided by Zuckerman and his colleagues (1962) when he divided subjects into three groups in order to study the specific effects of:

1. perceptive isolation in conjunction with confinement;
2. confinement alone, not in conjunction with perceptive isolation;
3. perceptive non-isolation in conjunction with non-confinement.

In terms of problem-solving ability, the findings indicate that the groups were not significantly different; important differences were found, however, in associational and inferential ability. Perceptive isolation seems to generate two types of effects: in an initial stage, a period of hyper-vigilance, with hallucinatory effects and claustrophobia observed; during a second stage there is a loss of interest in the sterile environment, an increase of attention to internal processes, a loss of orientation, diminution in the power of concentration, and an increase in anxiety and psychosomatic indisposition.

A study by Zubek and his collaborators (1963) sought to determine if the restriction of tactilo-kinesthetic stimulation alone brings about effects comparable to the ones described above; they, too, observed the appearance of bizarre thoughts and intellectual ineptitude, exaggerated emotional reactions, and a significant reduction of dexterity in perceptive-motor activities, but no significant differences in measures of intelligence.

Hebb's theory offers a framework for the interpretation of these findings. In summarizing the results of these studies, Bruner wrote (1961): "Perception and cognitive activity depend on a dynamically stable equilibrium based on contrasting or heterogeneous stimuli and on a shifting environment.''

The disorders observed in the above experiments with normal subjects were temporary, and disappeared shortly after the subjects' return to normal life conditions. This is possible when the period of sensory deprivation is relatively short, and when the subject can end the experiment at any time if he feels he has reached the limit of his physical or nervous resistance. Longer experiments, similar to the ones performed with animals, probably would provide more stable phenomena, but they obviously are not feasible.

Sensory restriction seems, then, to cause disturbances to the human adult; however, these disturbances do not effect cognitive processes in a systematic manner; rather, the major effects are on the perceptive-motor reactions and on the affective adaptation. Animal psychology has demonstrated that only the damages of early infancy result in lasting and practically irreversible deficiencies. Such experiments are impossible with children; therefore, a brief review will be made of infant studies which assessed the effects of infantile environment[1]. Following this, information derived from studies of sensory deficits, particularly those pertaining to the blind, will be reviewed.

The importance of a rich and varied environment for the developing infant has long been emphasized. Spitz (1945) attributed the deficiencies observed in children raised in hospitals or foster institutions to maternal deprivation. He also recognized the danger of excessive "hygienic" isolation of infants, and he recommended that the child be surrounded with objects which were apt to stimulate his visual sense and arouse in him exploratory and manipulative behavior patterns. Numerous experimental studies following Spitz's works confirmed and extended these suggestions.

The effect of educational conditions on the development of intelligence is the subject of a variety of research endeavors: comparative studies of identical twins raised together or separately, comparison of the intelligence of siblings, studies of children raised in conditions of deficient stimulation, etc. Although the results are not always clear; it is well established that the environmental conditions exert an influence on intellectual development and that the effect of this environmental influence is most noticeable when it occurs in infancy (Bloom, 1964).

Study of Sensory Deficits:
The Deaf and the Blind

Contributions from sensory pathology can be of value in the study of sensory deficiencies because they furnish information on the effect of sensory restriction on cognitive behaviors under relatively controllable conditions.

Study of the deaf

Most studies of sensory deficiency are concerned with *deaf children*. The loss of hearing, which completely deprives the child of externally generated auditory stimulation, also deprives him of the essential tool of cognition: language. Therefore, the relationships between language and thought, language and intelligence,

---

[1] In fact, the author would limit herself simply to saying that there is an abundance of studies utilizing other methods which touch on a question close to the one that she has raised.

language and concepts formation, etc., have been the foci of significant research. The obtained results generally verify a deficiency in the "conceptual thought" of the young deaf, a deficiency which is manifest in experiments requiring manipulation of mental abstractions (Oleron, 1951; Vincent, 1957). In most instances the deaf subjects performed at Oleron's "perceptual" level as opposed to the conceptual level, since they are deprived of language as a symbolic instrument; also it is harder for them to pass from one level to another than it is for a person who can hear.

There is difficulty, however, in utilizing these results in our study of the effects of sensory deprivations on cognitive processes, because in research on the deaf it is impossible to dissociate the roles played by the deprivation of language as a symbolic instrument from the deprivation of sensory stimulation. However, study of the organization of visual perception in the deaf does supply material of value to our problem. Indeed, if deafness results in a general deficiency, conceptual or intellectual, and if cognitive processes influence perceptive structures as many maintain, especially Piaget, then it should be quite interesting to review the behavior of deaf subjects in purely perceptive experiments and also in more complex experiments which involve spatial relations. In an experiment using the tachistoscope, the performance of deaf subjects was found to be equivalent to that of hearing ones (Oleron, 1950); but when performance of the two groups was compared on a more complex experiment involving discrimination of superimposed geometric forms, the deaf subjects were systematically inferior to the hearing ones (Oleron, 1964). Here again, though, interpretation of the role of language must be considered.

In research on the particular effects of sensory deprivation on cognitive processes, studies on blindness present certain advantages over those on deafness. For one thing, sight constitutes one of the principal means of appraising the exterior world and visual stimuli are by far the most numerous and the most varied; for another, although deprived of vision, the blind acquire language without difficulty. This is not the case with deaf children.

Study of the blind

Sight and cognition are so closely interrelated in the popular mind that "to see" is equated with "to know" or "to understand." This is why prejudices linking blindness with mental retardation have long prevailed, just as though the loss of sight rendered impossible any intellectual acquisition. As if to counter these misconceptions, others ascribe to the blind exceptional endowments in the manual, intellectual, and moral fields; at times, blindness has even been considered a sign of divine illumination (Villey, 1927; Henry, 1958). Progress in the education and the instruction of the blind, as well as in education of the public, has served to develop conceptions more in accord with reality.

Consideration will now be given to the development of language in the blind, to the development of intelligence as measured by general tests, and finally to the development of "conceptual thought."

1. *Language*: There is unanimous agreement on one point: blindness does not interfere with the acquisition of language by the young child. These conclusions derive from the extended study by Norris, Spaulding, and Brodie (1957), and from one by Maxfield and Buchholz (1957). When the latter adapted the Vineland Scale of Social Maturity for use with the blind they found it unnecessary to revise the language items; norms established for the sighted were appropriate. Unless the possibility of the imitation of the phonatory movements of mouth and lips is to be considered, sight does not seem to be a major contribution to speech production. To our knowledge, Miner (1963) is the only person to observe a higher percentage of language deficiency among visually-impaired subjects than among sighted ones (33% vs. 6%); even then, a majority of these deficiencies were articulatory.

If one agrees that the mechanisms for the acquisition and development of language in the blind do not differ from those in the sighted, then the basis for language should be the same in both groups. "Verbalism," (which educators seek to correct) is defined as an excess of verbal concepts not supported by any concrete perceptive awareness, which promotes language deformations (Cutsforth, 1951; Henry, 1948; Harley, 1963).

2. *I.Q. Scores*: When mental tests are adapted for use with the blind on the assumption that their linguistic functions are unimpaired, extensive use is made of oral communication. While intelligence tests for the deaf consist generally of manipulation without need for verbal expression, tests designed to measure the intelligence of the blind generally are verbal.

Although the Terman test was first adapted for use with the visually-impaired in 1916 (Haines), it was uncontestably Hayes who made the major contribution in this domain. He provided three successive adaptations of the Terman scale, and the Interim Hayes Test (1943), continues to be widely used as a measure of intelligence for the blind. When he combined Forms L and M of the Terman–Merrill, Hayes eliminated all the tests which required vision, and retained only the purely verbal ones: vocabulary, verbal absurdities, similarities, memory, arithmetic, etc. The test was standardized on more than 500 blind subjects at the Perkins School for the Blind. No adjustment was required in the ages at which high scores were achieved on the various items: i.e., the blind subjects scored well on the verbal items of the Terman–Merrill at the same age as the sighted. The mean I.Q. obtained by Hayes for the blind was approximately 100; but the range was greater among the blind subjects, mainly because an increased number of them were mentally retarded.

Similar results are obtained when the verbal scale of the Wechsler–Bellevue test is used without any adaptation. Here, again, the verbal mean I.Q. of the blind is approximately 100, but the dispersion is greater than for the sighted.

Statistically, these facts show that blindness does not imply disorders in intellectual development as it is defined by these tests. Today it is established that there is no causal relationship between mental retardation and blindness, but when the two handicaps are concomitant, they may have a common etiology — e.g., maternal rubella during pregnancy, encephalitis, etc. — or it may be coincidence (the blindness being genetic).

Except as a general indicator, it is difficult to use the findings of Hayes in the present study, since his group was comprised not only of the congenitally blind but also of the adventitiously blind and the partially sighted, some of whom were even able to read printed characters. Such a sampling may be justified within the framework of a particular line of study. The questions to be answered in the present study concern the congenitally blind only.

Although his data are derived from a heterogeneous sample, one of Hayes' findings is of interest. In trying to analyse the patterns of successes and failures in blind subjects, Hayes observed lowered performance on items related to "reflection and reasoning"—e.g., comprehension, analogies, similarities, etc.—but not on memory items (Hayes, 1941; 1950). In the last few years, the writer administered the French version of the Interim Hayes–Binet Test to approximately 600 visually-impaired persons and, observed a similar pattern.

An adaptation attempted by Langan (1945) is interesting not only because of its aim but also because it failed to prove its point. Questioning the Hayes–Binet's exclusively verbal character, Langan revised the Form L of the Terman–Merrill, and replaced items requiring the use of sight by similar ones requiring tactual manipulation only: bead-stringing, peg-board reproduction of geometric structures, object assembly, etc. A British standardization of this adaptation involved some 300 blind children, ages five to 16. Like Hayes, Langan found it unnecessary to make age adjustments on verbal items; however, the "performance" items were successfully performed by the blind children at a much later age than by the sighted. For instance, the reproduction with sticks of a square or rhombus was accomplished by the blind between eight and 12 years, and by the sighted between four and six years. The same age discrepancy existed for almost every non-verbal item.

If a subject had even a slight degree of residual vision the test was invalid. It was also invalid if used with the adventitiously blind; frequently, in these persons, prior visual experience enhances performance on non-verbal items. A number of adventitiously blind were used in the tests—the exact number is not known. They obtained higher I.Q.'s than the congenitally blind. However, we are not in a position to interpret this superiority, except as confirmation of the findings of studies described earlier.

Along the same lines is a Japanese adaptation of Kohs' Block Design Test proposed by Ohwaki (1960). Instead of being colored, the different sides of the cubes were covered with a particular texture: there then was a combination of textures at the tactual perception level, rather than a combination of colors at the visual perception level as used by Kohs. Without regard for standardization or other statistical information, Ohwaki's adaptation of this test was presented as "a measure of non-verbal intelligence of the blind." Unfortunately, the Kohs test was saturated with spatial factors as well as with relational aspects of intelligence, and this combination makes it difficult to analyze the performance of subjects who have mental disorders—e.g., schizophrenia, brain damage, senile deterioration, etc.—and especially of those who have language disorders. We have strong reason to think that its adaptation further strengthens spatial interferences and adds an element of manual dexterity that is much greater than in the visual test. Because of these circumstances it is not surprising to find that the mean I.Q. of the blind, as measured by Ohwaki's adaptation, was only 84. Should it be referred to as a measure of intelligence when there are so many uncontrolled and uncontrollable variables, e.g., perception, spatial organization, and motor ability?

To complete the review of literature on the general intellectual development of the blind, review is made of the study by Norris, Spaulding, and Brodie (1957) on the development of blind infants and pre-school children. Using the Maxfield–Fjeld Social Maturity Scale, the non-visual items of the Gesell and Cattell tests, plus the Interim Hayes–Binet Test for the older children, they observed that the psychological development of the pre-school blind child is exactly comparable to that of the sighted, except for delays occurring in the areas of fine motor coordination and locomotion. Generally, blind children started walking between the ages of one-and-a-half to four years. Eighty percent (80%) of the 300 sample subjects were totally blind.

In summary, the above data establish that when exclusively verbal tests are used— e.g., Binet vocabulary, comprehension, analogy, memory, etc.—the average development of the blind and visually impaired is similar to that of the sighted, but the variability is greater. Data on "performance" tests are more complex since these tests cause disturbances that we are not in a position to interpret, and which leads us back to the problems discussed in the first part of this chapter. There is need to determine if the difficulties encountered by the blind are the result of perceptual, spatial, or motor insufficiencies, or of deficiencies in intellectual—"operative"—processes.

3. *Conceptual Thought*: This term most often involves the classificatory processes. Three studies in this field must be noted. The first, by McAndrew (1948), compared normal, blind, and deaf subjects in terms of rigidity and plasticity of behavior. McAndrew hypothesized a positive correlation between rigidity and social isolation, and, indeed, in a classificatory test, behavior of the deaf subjects was more rigid than that of the blind; in turn, behavior of the blind subjects was more rigid than that of the sighted subjects.

Later Axelrod (1959), observed that experiments comparing the blind and the sighted typically used tasks which, in varying degrees involved, spatial relations; therefore, he sought to determine if the deficient performance exhibited by the congenitally blind is specific to spatial representation and "visualization" (Worchel, 1951) or if the deficiency also is manifest in "conceptual" or "abstract" tasks. To determine this, he used a tactual classification and a generalization test. On the classification test there were no major differences between blind and blindfolded sighted subjects; however, on a classification test which also involved transfer, performance of the congenitally blind subjects was significantly inferior to that of the adventitiously blind and of the sighted subjects. To interpret these results, Axelrod referred to Hebb's theory on the importance of a rich and stimulating environment during infancy; difficulties encountered by the congenitally blind indicate that early perceptive restriction is manifested in generally inferior functioning even in tasks not solely based on spatialization and visual representation.

In subsequent chapters the research of McAndrew and Axelrod, will be reviewed and their interpretations discussed in the light of the findings of our own experimental researches.

In the third study, Rubin (1964) compared three matched groups of subjects, ages 18 to 49: (1) 25 congenitally blind, (2) 25 adventitiously blind, who had sight through their twelfth year, and (3) 25 sighted. To make the comparison, four "abstraction" tests were used: the similarities sub-test of the Wechsler Adult Intelligence Scale (WAIS), a proverbs test, the Kahn Test of Symbol Arrangement (which involves classification of objects on varying criteria) and a completion test involving numerical series. Performance of the congenitally blind group was significantly inferior to that of the adventitiously blind and of the sighted on the proverbs test. Although similar tendencies were noted on the other two tests, the differences were not statistically significant. In drawing the conclusion that congenital blindness creates particular difficulties in the realm of abstraction and on the formation of concepts, Rubin agrees with Cutsforth (1951), Lowenfeld (1955), and Omwake and Solnit (1961).

Summary and Conclusion

From presently available data can one state precisely the effects of sensory deprivation on cognitive processes? Animal studies can be used to illustrate the systematic inferiority of groups raised in conditions of poor stimulation—e.g., sensory deprivation and environmental deficiency. Experiments on human adults are less conclusive. They emphasize the behavioral disorders (hallucinations, poor concentration, psychosomatic ailments, errors in perception and memory, etc.) that follow temporary sensory deprivation. The deterioration of symbolic functions does not always accompany these manifestations.

Therefore, conclusive evidence is not available on this particular point. Although the experimental conditions in which certain studies have been carried out are not always acceptable, we can nonetheless consider the following points:

1. Normal language development occurs in the blind;

2. On verbal intelligence tests, the mean I.Q. of the blind is approximately normal—i.e., 100—but the dispersion of the scores is greater than for the sighted because mental retardation and blindness frequently are concomitant conditions;

3. Scores for the congenitally blind on non-verbal or "performance" tests are difficult to interpret. We do not know whether the difficulties are due entirely to perceptual-motor factors, which are always present, or whether they actually indicate symbolic and logical deficiencies;

4. An interesting indication is provided by three studies of conceptual thought (McAndrew, 1948; Axelrod, 1959; and Rubin, 1964) that reported minor but systematic inferiority of the congenitally blind in comparison to the sighted.

From these data, the problem will be defined and clarified, along with the general theory that includes the writer's own experimental work.

Chapter Two

SENSORY DEPRIVATION AND INTELLIGENCE:
Statement of the Problem and Working Hypotheses

Statement of the Problem

The variety of limitations imposed by blindness has been considered in the preceding historical and bibliographical review. Early deprivation of sight limits stimulation from the environment in a manner which is quantitative as well as qualitative.

Quantitative: Because visual observations are both inclusive and simultaneous, and also because the visual field of observation is vast, vision is the individual's major channel of information on the objects surrounding him. Consequently, visual deprivation represents a loss in the variety and in the quantity of perceptual stimuli normally apprehended by the human organism. Review of the literature concerned with the characteristics of tactilo-kinesthetic perception has shown that this sensory mode is less "effective" and less efficient when there is visual impairment.

Qualitative: We have seen also that the level of organization of tactilo-kinesthetic perceptions is quite inferior to that of the organization of visual perceptions. The limited scope of tactual apprehension, its successive and fragmentary character and the need for a final synthesis to restore the wholeness of objects make spatial relations difficult to apprehend and data difficult to structure when the tactile mode of perception is employed.

Early visual deprivation alters the child's contact with the outside world and diminishes the perceptive constraint exerted on the individual by external reality. In the present study it is this aspect of early blindness which is of major concern, and which will characterize our experimental group of blind persons.

However, an observation of primary importance must be made at this point.

Perceptive impoverishment is not the only consequence of blindness. There are also limitations in exploratory and social experiences and, generally, the affective realm also is impaired. The trauma caused by the birth of a disabled infant tends to create a family atmosphere which is less than optimum for the blind child. Lack of information concerning child-rearing practices for the blind generates over-protective family attitudes. In turn, these place even greater limitations on the child's contact with the outside world. For example, fear of possible "accidents" frequently causes parents to restrict the child's activities.

If we concentrate on the changes in cognition accompanying blindness, it does not mean that we think that such a change is the same with all subjects. It varies with family atmosphere, and is not necessarily inevitable or irremediable: it can be attenuated by suitable educational methods. Its presence, allowing for differences in family background, constitutes the only element common to all the subjects in our experimental group.

The same is true for the affective adaptation of our young subjects. We have been unable to control this, within the limited framework of our study. Its effects are similar to those of sensory privation in that they disturb the child's contact with the outside world (there is a general tendency towards introversion among the blind).

The present study seeks to determine the effects that sensory deprivation has on the acquisition of knowledge and more particularly on the formation of the cognitive structures of the blind individual. Does a major reduction of perceptive knowledge interfere with intellectual processes? Or, stated differently, what is the role played by perceptive data in the development of the child's logical reasoning?

There is need at this point to define "intellectual development," since different and even contradictory theories and definitions do exist. Therefore, an indication of the general theoretical framework used for the present study provided.

Although a complete review of the various theories of intelligence is not attempted, mention will be made of the three which seem to have had marked influence on contemporary psychology.

"General Intelligence" and Determination of the I.Q.

We have already seen how comprehensive tests derived from the Binet-Simon Scale have been adapted for use with the blind. Can a simple measure of the verbal or performance intellectual quotient of visually-impaired individuals be sufficient to determine the effects of sensory deficiency on the development of intelligence? From the perspective in which we have placed our study, the answer clearly is no.

The purpose of comprehensive verbal tests is to promote interplay between different aspects of mental activity. Tests of short-term memory, vocabulary, and comprehension of social situations as well as logical reasoning measures such as similarities, absurd sentences, and logical comprehension, are tests which are directly related to elements of social and academic learning, e.g., arithmetic, days of the week, months of the year, etc. The total score does not provide information on the distribution of successes and failures in different areas. Nonetheless, it is that distribution that concerns us or, more exactly, it is the effect of blindness on cognitive processes rather than on social or school insufficiencies, that is our critical focus.

Problem–solving

Although problem-solving ability is a very important factor in the psychology of intelligence it is not from this angle that we propose to approach the study of intellectual development in blind youths. Reasons for this are threefold:

First, the definition of problem-situations is difficult. We have examined a proliferation of these situations in the literature of contemporary psychology and the concept has been greatly extended. Oleron considers a problem to be "any situation in which the subject's immediately available repertory of responses fails to provide appropriate reactions" (1963, p. 38). In other words, a problem exists when a new response — an "invention" — is called for, a response not in the previous repertory of the subject. However, it can be considered as a problem-situation only when a solution is attainable (an abstract equation does not constitute a problem for a six-year-old child). Moreover, the solution must be arrived at by intellectual means, not by motor activity or learning.

Oleron noted, however, that despite these criteria, or rather because of their very general character, the number of problem-situations is virtually unlimited. Since it has not been possible to define and analyze the intervening psychological processes there is no general theory of problem-solving.

Secondly, a genetic, or developmental, scale of problem-solving behaviors is not available, undoubtedly because of the lack of a homogeneous theoretical background. Such a scale would arrange given behaviors in the order of their appearance in the course of the child's development.

Finally, in most problem-situations, the responses to them are regarded either as "success" or "failure," depending on whether or not a practical result is obtained, such as the opening or closing of a door. By contrast, the present study seeks to observe intellectual or rational behavior as it is manifest in logical reasoning situations that can be qualified as "true" or "false." The question is: "Does the alteration of contact which occurs between the blind individual and the outside reality modify the nature of the "logical truth?" Or does it merely alter the age for its attainment? Or does it, perhaps, have no effect?

To speak of the logical structure of intellectual thought is to refer to Piaget's theory, a theory that offers a general conceptual framework within which to define the relations between organism and environment, or, more specifically, between intellectual and perceptive processes. It also provides detailed descriptions of the genetic steps in the formation of logical thought structures. For this reason Piaget's theory is the one used in this study.

Theoretical Framework: Piaget's Theory of Intelligence

The present study does not intend to offer a comprehensive review of Piaget's theory of intelligence but it does provide some of the definitions and concepts which will be used in the statement of our hypothesis, in the arrangement of the experiments, and in the general interpretation of the results.

The Intellectual Processes and the Operational Aspects of Thought

The adaptative nature of intelligence

The starting point for Piaget's theory is found in the continuity he sees between the biological processes of adaptation of the organism to its environment and the psychological processes of the intelligence which assure the structuring of this environment.

Every organism lives and develops through a series of exchanges with the surrounding environment. Two mechanisms are basic to these exchanges; (1) *assimilation*, a process by which outside materials are coordinated and internalized, and (2) *accommodation,* a process caused by the exertion of environmental pressures on the organism (phenotypical variations, according to the biologists).

According to Piaget, this defninition of biological adaptation also applies to intelligence, which merely constitutes "a particular instance of organic activity." Psychologically, there is assimilation when the data from experience are incorporated into existing schemes or mental structures. Reciprocally, there is accommodation when existing schemes are modified in order to incorporate new elements the environment acts on the organism. It can be said that accommodation occurs when, in incorporating new elements into the external structure, the intelligence modifies the latter to adapt them to new data. Accommodation is a differentiation in one's response to the action of objects on existing structures already established by the subject. The double process of assimilation of outside data to the existing framework of thought, and of accommodation to the always new elements of reality is basic to the intellectual activity of the individual (Piaget, 1960).

Definition of intelligence

Biological adaptation, or the *direct interpretration between organism and environment, extends into mental life and gives rise to intellectual adaptations which is grounded in the mediated exchanges between subject and objects.* As development proceeds, these exchanges occur at increasingly longer spatial-temporal distances, and follow more and more complex paths. The final equilibrium toward which all these exchanges tend is a structure within the interrelated processes of thought, characterized by its *reversible* mobility. By contrast, the initial sensory-motor elementary adaptations are rigid, static, and unidirectional.

Reversibility of thought processes also constitutes the main aspect of logical operations. The intellectual processes are organized by the same laws that define logical organizations. Piaget's theory of intelligence is an *operatory theory:* i.e., intelligence is considered as a system of "operations" organized in "general structures" which do not become fully operational until the end of a long and slow genetic process. Analysis of the steps and mechanisms of this genetic process constitutes the central aspect of the psychological study of intelligence, a study which starts with the elementary sensory-motor adaptations and continues to the most elaborated forms of logical thought and mathematics.

What is an "operation"? It is an *"interiorized and reversible action* which, with other interdependent operations, forms a structure characterized by laws effected by both forms of reversibility" (Piaget, *Perceptive Mechanisms*, 1961, p. 441). Initially, the terms used in this definition will be analyzed; later, attention will be directed to the genetic formation of these operations.

An *interiorized action* is a "mental (or interior) action performed on symbolic objects either by representation and application to mental images of objects, or by direct application to symbolic systems (words, etc.)" (Piaget, 1957, p. 44).

Thus, either effective or interiorized action is the essential element of an operation. While an action is a necessary condition for an operation, it is not a sufficient one and all actions are not operations. Piaget speaks of *"operative* structures" when referring to a grouping of real or virtual actions which precede an operation as well as the actions which reach the operatory level, but his use of the term *"operatory structures"* generally is more limited, as the following definition indicates:

"Actions combine and form operations," writes Piaget, "as soon as their coordination reaches the level of reversible composition" (1950, p. 209). *Reversibility,* which is a compensation for the transformations taking place, is in fact the essential characteristic of operatory systems. It is defined as "the ability to execute the same action in opposite directions with full awareness that it is only one action" (Piaget, 1957, p. 44). If there is no awareness that it is the same action in reverse, then reversibility has not been achieved, and we have an empirical return to the starting point.

When this level of reversibility is attained, a set of qualitatively new characters replaces the one-way actions of the previous level. Operations are coordinated in general systems which allow for passage from one operation to another within the same operatory grouping. This is done according to the laws of composition which govern logical structures.

Steps in the construction of functional thought

Because Piaget's stages of cognitive development are known generally, only a brief review will be furnished in the present writing.

The *sensory-motor stage* which occupies the period from birth to 18 months, approximately, is characterized by the progressive formation of sensory-motor schemes. For Piaget, "the scheme" of an action is "the general structure of this action which is consolidated through exercise, and applies itself to different situations as they are encountered in the environment" (1960, p. 552). Piaget also terms "sensory-motor" activities those in which "only perceptions, attitudes, and movements intervene." Sensory-motor intelligence is "the capacity to resolve practical problems through activities prior to language acquisition" (Piaget, 1957, p. 46).

The progressive coordination of sensory-motor schemes leads to the construction of certain "invariants" such as object permanence or spatial organization (i.e., "grouping of displacements" in which two displacements of inverse direction cancel each other and bring about a return to the starting point).

The *preconceptual period,* which generally extends from 18 or 20 months to four years, is marked by the development of language and symbolic functions. Imitation, particularly "deferred" imitation, constitutes for Piaget the transitional element between sensory-motor schemas and representative thought. The transition starts with deferred imitation, and proceeds through progressive interiorization. Thus symbolic images are formed.

During the *intuitive period,* which occupies the period from four to seven years, approximately, a gradual coordination of symbolic representations lead the child to the threshold of operations. Intuition or "action executed in thought" is figurative thought and is more refined than preconceptual thought in that it deals with wider configurations. Intuition, however, continues to utilize symbolic imagery and still carries with it part of its inherent limitations. Consequently, at this level, intelligence remains "prelogical": i.e., it is capable only of actions which are short, unidirectional, dependent on figurative representation, and centered on some aspect of reality.

The progressive articulation of intuitions makes possible short-term relations between one or two elements, but relations established in this manner are still unable to form groups by themselves. "At this level, however, the identity of the various elements involved in the course of actions is not clear, nor is there conservation of the groups involved in the actions: i.e., there is neither deduction nor real operation" (Piaget, 1947, p. 165).

Intuition leads to decentration and in doing so promotes the coordination of viewpoints, towards reversible mobility and operations.

The period of *concrete operations,* which generally extends from the seventh or eighth to the eleventh or twelfth year, is characterized by the progressive attainment of the *mobile and reversible equilibrium* required for "groupings." The child's thought is no longer centered on states, but on the successive transformations which connect the different perceived states one to the other. Through these groupings an equilibrium is achieved between assimilation and accommodation, which originally acted in the opposite way (distorting assimilation and phenotypic accommodation of intuitive thought).

At approximately 10 years, the child reaches a plateau in equilibration which is marked by the relative completion of notions basic to the comprehension of space, time, physical invariants, classifications, seriations, numbers, etc. However, the operations formed in this manner are limited to the "concrete" level; they deal with manipulated objects, either perceivable or imaginable. They cannot be applied to all subjects nor to all reasoning.

Because of their "concrete" character, these operations do not justify any simple verbal hypotheses; instead, they are tied to reality, a reality which is progressively structured by their actions.

The final stage is termed *formal operations*. Just as the transition to concrete operations required (at the representational level) a reconstruction of acquisitions of the sensory-motor period, the transition from concrete operations to formal operations requires transposition of concrete groupings to a subsequent level which level is characterized by hypothetico-deductive thought, thought liberated from concrete content and capable of reasoning on propositions. Before acting on objects, such thought builds an ensemble of hypotheses from which a choice will be made. "From now on, facts are conceived as effective realizations emerging from a universe of possible transformations, ... they are explained or admitted as facts only after being submitted to a verification process which takes into consideration the ensemble of possible hypotheses consistent with the given situation" (Piaget and Inhelder, 1959, p. 220).

Formal thought, then, is characterized by reasoning based on verbal statements rather than on concrete manipulations. This does not mean that every verbal thought is a formal thought; at age seven or eight it is possible to engage in simple verbal reasoning provided it is tied to well-established concrete representations. When the subject is unable to translate given propositions into figurative representations, he has to deal in hypotheses and make use of the *logic of propositions*. The most classic illustration of this decalage between concrete operations and formal operations is the famous Burt Test: Edith's hair is lighter than Suzanne's, and Edith's hair is darker than Lili's; which has the darkest hair of the three?" It is answered successfully at 11 or 12 years, while the concrete operation corresponding to it, seriation of asymmetrical transitive relations, is achieved around age seven or eight.

These, then, are the main steps through which the individual progresses from primitive sensory-motor operations to superior forms of thought and reasoning.

Logico-mathematical operations and infralogical operations

From seven or eight years onward, according to Piaget, two kinds of operations are taking form: logico-mathematical operations and infralogical operations. "Logico-mathematical" operations are those which establish relations between given objects (e.g., classifications, seriations, numbers — particularly similarities and differences) or relations which are independent of the spatio-temporal arrangement of the objects on which the operation is bearing.

On the contrary, "infralogical" operations are those which tend to construct the object itself, however extended it may be in terms of space and time. Unlike logico-mathematical operations, they do not derive from relations based on the similarities or differences between objects, but from relations based on the proximity and relative position between the different parts of an object.

The ambiguous term "infralogical" must not be confused with "pre-logical," which refers to the pre-operatory thought level in which reversible groupings have not yet been achieved. "Infralogical" operations as characterized by Piaget are not "less logical" than logico-mathematical operations; both are *operations*: i.e., mobile and reversible structures that can form by themselves. Infralogical operations and logico-mathematical are both achieved at approximately seven or eight years; both depend on the same mechanisms of thought. They differ only in the kind of relations which they set in motion. While logico-mathematical operations group objects into classes and sub-classes, infralogical operations group parts into a whole, and make possible seriations and relationships based on order or spatial location. (Piaget, 1950).

The distinction which Piaget makes between logico-mathematical operations and infralogical operations is useful because in these two cases the relationship between operations, particularly concrete operations, and perceptive structures is not the same. Piaget distinguishes the "operative" aspect of thought from the "figurative" aspect (perceptions and figurative representations).

The role of language

According to Piaget, the operatory development cannot be entirely explained by the existence of language. Language contains logical structures, which are passed on ready made to the child. These structures will not be properly integrated and interpreted by him until corresponding but independent operatory systems have been formed in another way. The origin of operations occurs not in language but in sensory-motor activity which generates the schemes of assimilation. Piaget (1963) bases his theory of operatory development on the following facts:

1. During the first 18 to 20 months of life a logic of action occurs and characterizes sensory-motor intelligence prior to the acquisition of language;

2. Although language generally is acquired between two and four years, it is not until the approximate age of nine or 10 that the child becomes capable of a logical handling of the concepts which it conveys;

3. Even though his language is generally normal, the educable mentally retarded child generally does not proceed beyond the level of concrete operations (Inhelder, 1943);

4. Research carried out in Geneva by Ajuriaguerra and Inhelder on the operatory development of young children suffering from language disorder has shown that, despite a level comprehension and verbal expressions far below average, 70 percent of the children could, according to Ajuriaguerra (1963) "...be considered as having achieved a normal overall operatory level" (1963, p. 162). ("Overall" level seems to be defined by conservation assessments.) Even on tests dealing with the formation of "conceptual thought," which involve semi-verbal tasks and the classification and seriation of manipulable materials, 46 to 66 percent of the subjects exhibited normal or superior performance. In other words, despite grave deficiencies in language, approximately half of those tested attained a normal concrete operatory level. On the other hand, important deficits were found in spatial representation

and figurative anticipation. Because of these findings, Inhelder hypothesized that, in these subjects, language deficiency constitutes only one, (but perhaps the most visible) aspect of a more general symbolic-figurative deficiency (1963a).

5. In studies of deaf persons, which should have been decisive, the results obtained are not comparable. Borelli (1951) observed the deaf have only a slight retardation in tests of concrete seriation and of corresponding placement of two series. On the other hand, Oleron and Herren (1961) observed a considerable delay (approximately six years) in the acquisition by the deaf of conservation of weight and of number. Even allowing for certain technical factors which could have increased the difficulties for the deaf, the fact remains that in comparison to non-hearing impaired subjects their deficits are significant. Oleron holds that these results indicate a tendency of the deaf to accept whatever is perceived, whereas the hearing subject, who also uses verbal concepts, is more successful in disengaging himself from the concrete plane.

Piaget refers to the experimental studies currently carried out by Affolther, which employ techniques different from those used by Oleron and Herren. In these studies, which are concerned with concrete logical operations, the deaf subjects are found to be slightly inferior to the hearing ones, but the deficiencies are much less than those reported by Oleron.

Although from a Piegetian perspective, language is neither a necessary nor a sufficient condition for the development of concrete logical operations, it may, "perhaps," be necessary for progression to the formal level of thought. It comprises a symbolic system whose possibilities can be truly exhausted by a child only when he already has acquired by other means the logical structures necessary for its manipulation.

The Figurative Aspect of Thought

In opposition to the "operative" aspect which, as we have seen, relates to transformations and actions, and thus to anything that modifies the object, the "figurative" aspect of representation refers to configurations and states derived from perception and mental imagery.

Perception

While Gestalt psychology tends to assume a direct relation between perception and intelligence, the dualist position is one in which perception and intelligence are radically opposed. Discarding both, Piaget adopts an attitude, which he calls "interactionist," in which he notes a number of differences and similarities between perception and intelligence.

Piaget posits that the *differences* between perception and intelligence result essentially from the fact that intellectual structures organize themselves in "groupings," while perceptive structures do not correspond to any of the conditions which characterize such groupings. At the perceptual level, there is neither additivity (the whole is different from the sum of the parts) nor reversibility of compositions, nor associativity, nor identity of an element to itself through varying relational placings. When intelligence compares two terms with each other, neither the "comparing" nor the "compared" is deformed by the comparison. On the contrary, at the perceptual level, and particularly with primary perceptions, Piaget has shown there is a "standard error": i.e., that any fixed element ("standard") is overrated in comparison to others. In a more general fashion, centration, which is defined as being "a single fixation of one's eyes" (Piaget, 1963, p. 4), causes visual deformations or perceptual illusions. These deformations are counter-balanced, in part, by successive centrations — or "decentrations" — but the successive visual focal point, unlike intellectual processes, does not exhaust all possible combinations. Centrations are distributed according to a probabilistic system which involves "meetings" and "couplings." Their relatively fortuitous character explains the absence of composition and the irreversibility of perceptual structures (Piaget, 1977, pp. 93–95; 1961).

Analogies between perceptual structures and intellectual structures do exist, however; both imply constructive activity on the part of the subject. In effect, if the primary perceptive structures are essentially statistical in nature and cannot form by themselves, *perceptual activity* — i.e., "the establishment of relations between elements perceived in different fields" (Piaget, 1963, p. 16) — progressively guides and coordinates centrations and reduces the role of chance. In this manner, perceptual activity introduces a coordination in the perceptual structures and a progressive ability toward composition. In fact, it leads to the elaboration of "perceptual schemes" which constitute the ensemble of relationships that perceptive activity can recognize (decentrations, transfers, transpositions, etc.) within the perceived object.

Furthermore, perceptual activities develop in correlation with (and represent only one special aspect of) sensory-motor schemes, and are differentiated in terms of the various kinds of perceptions. "The only difference between perceptual and sensory-motor activities comes from the fact that the former are specialized according to the diverse sensory organs (eye movements, etc.), while the latter touch upon multi-sensory realities and cause the entire action to come into play, especially through eye-hand coordination" (Piaget, 1957, p. 73).

Under such conditions, perception as a "particular case of sensory-motor activities in general" could not furnish a starting point for cognition or understanding, nor could there be a direct relation between perceptual processes and intellectual ones. However, perception and intelligence *do have a common origin,* which is none other than the sensory-motor scheme that functions at the level of perceptual activities and which also characterizes the first manifestations of intelligence in the new-born child.

If perceptions like these are not yet cognition, what is their place in the acquisition of knowledge? Since they are oriented towards a "maximum accommodation" (Piaget, 1957, p. 103), they play the role of indicators, of *signifiers* on which the schematizing assimilation that attributes meanings will function.

"From the epistemological viewpoint, perception constitutes a system of cues, or "signifiers," which are fortuitously obtained through relationships which are established by sensory-motor activity; as these cues are assigned significations, relationships are established; *the perceptual or sensory element is only the signifier; the motor activity provides signification:* i.e., static cues guide the possible or real transformations carried out by sensory-motor activity" (Piaget, 1950, p. 183).

The role of perceptual cues, characterized by a "signifier," is again found at the level of mental imagery.

Mental Imagery

As symbolic functioning emerges around age 18 to 20 months, it makes possible a differentiation between signifiers and signified. Piaget posits that *imitation* assures the transition between sensory-motor activities and representation. "At the sensory-motor level, imitation consists chiefly of a representation by gesture, which is quite different from the mental representation which will occur later." In line with Guillaume, Wallon, and the French psychological tradition, Piaget accords imitation a place of importance in the transition from the perceived to the represented.

Discarding the old conception which made the image a passive copy of the object and a simple extension of perception, Piaget hypothesized that the image is an "interiorized imitation" and that through a genetic relation *figurative symbolism is constituted from imitative mechanisms.* For instance, the representation of a sound of a gesture will be accompanied by a *"rough effort to produce it,"* and the visual image is the extension "not of perception as a receptive mechanism, but of the sensory-motor explorative activity which follows the outlines of the object" (Piaget, 1960, p. 562).

Imitation tends to be a *copy of reality,* a copy which is by no means passive, but which, quite to the contrary, constitutes the purest case of accommodation of the subject to exterior objects. Because it essentially involves a reproduction of reality, actual or mental, imitation tends to be static. It is centered on states and not on transformations, transformations which provide unity and internal coherence to objects by connecting the different states. Symbolic imagery presents, therefore, neither mobility nor reversibility. Its preponderance at the pre-operatory level (which Piaget even terms "abusive," 1960, p. 557) constitutes the main obstacle to logical reasoning.

Mental imagery facilitates operatory development by serving in both playful and conceptual activity as a *symbolizer* to which significations will be assigned through the process of assimilation. In other words, although it is but on another plane (the plane of figurative representation), the symbolic signifier which will serve the actions and transformations proper to operativity.

Since the image is an "interiorized imitation," and since, in a general manner, figurative symbolism is established from imitative mechanisms, it becomes evident that this form of representation of reality also has its origin in the sensory-motor schematization that imitation extends by adding to it the new, and irreducible, aspect of figurative representation. Thus as in perceptual structures we find once again that sensory-motor schemes and activities are the point of origin of cognition.

The characteristics of figurative structures which distinguish them from operative structures of thought are:

1. Figurative structures (perceptions and mental imagery) are static, rarely reversible and generally unrelated, because they are centered on states, not on transformations. By contrast, operative structures are mobile and reversible and bear on transformations between two states;

2. Like verbal symbols, figurative structures play the role of signifier to which operative structures, through generalizing assimilation and coordination of actions, will assign significations;

3. Figurative structures are oriented toward a copy of reality: i.e., toward "maximum accommodation" to environmental conditions. On the contrary, operative structures realize an equilibrium between assimilation and accommodation;

4. Finally, figurative structures draw their origin from sensory-motor schemes which involve either perceptive activities or imitation. Because operative structures also have their origin in the sensory-motor schemes, there is a common origin from which both forms of thought progressively develop.

Relations Between the Figurative and Operative Aspects of Thought

The emphasis placed by Piaget on operativity readily indicates a *subordination of the figurative to the operative* in intellectual activities.

Perceptual structures and figurative representations never precede operations and it is operatory development which grants them the relative mobility which they achieve at more advanced levels. For instance, the figurative representation of the transformation of an arc into á straight line — by stretching — or of the intermediary positions taken by a stem passing from the vertical to the horizontal position, is only possible when operatory coordinations have already organized these transformations into mobile and reversible systems. Figurative representation and, above all, figurative anticipation are adequate only when corresponding operatory systems have already been organized.

Mental imagery in logico-mathematical and infralogical operations: Distinction has been made between logico-mathematical and infralogical operations (see pp. 00–00) because the relations between each of these two operations and figurative structures in general are not precisely the same, at least at the concrete level. Logico-mathematical operations are the operations which establish relationships *between* distinct objects—classifications, seriations, numbers—while infralogical operations are the ones which tend to *constitute the object itself*—space and time.

Images which are basic to infralogical operations—e.g., spatial operations— more closely approximate the object of the operations than the images which are basic to logico-mathematical operations. Actually, there is no perception of a class, or of a relation or of a number; perception or images of a class are subjective in character, and tend to be removed from the corresponding concept. On the other hand, images basic to spatial operations are of the same nature as the operations themselves, for they both deal with the object itself: i.e., in the infralogical domain, the "symbolizer" (images) and the "symbolized" (represented reality) are of the same nature.

In another way, if one considers, on the one hand, the states between two transformations, which by simplifying characterize figurative structures, and, on the other hand, the transformations connecting two states, and which characterize operations, it appears that infralogical transformation—e.g, spatial or physical—just as well as the states themselves, can be represented on a figurative plane. Thus, an adequate figurative representation corresponds to operations which divide, stretch, displace, etc., but there could not be such an image for a numerical operation. Thus Piaget speaks of a "homogeneity of nature" between spatial images and spatial operations, a homogeneity which obviously does not exist in logico-mathematical operations.

The similarity of nature between the images and the object of spatial operations serves to explain the existence of a "geometrical intuition" which, according to Piaget, frequently but erroneously has been considered as possessing greater cognitive value than other forms of mental imagery. The relationship between spatial images and operations does not confer on the spatial domain any characteristics which are fundamentally different from other logical fields. Like logico-mathematical operations, spatial images are not more advanced than other corresponding operations. Because spatial images originate at the sensory-motor level their perceptual framework is limited, and any progress is guided and enriched by operations. As Piaget states, ". . . their figurative aspect becomes more and more subordinated to the operative aspect of thought, and the information provided reflects this subordination" (Piaget and Beth, 1961, p. 234).

According to Piaget, figurative structures play a supportive role in cognition: i.e., they provide the symbolic material on which operations will act, but the role is a secondary one, dependent on operative structures.

The Object–Subject Relation in Learning

As previously noted, figurative structures characterize the accommodation of the subject to environmental awareness: i.e., to a more acute differentiation of schemes which adapt them to the particular characters of objects. Consequently, does the subordination of the figurative to the operative signify a subordination of accommodation to operativity? Operativity itself is defined as an equilibrium between assimilatory mechanisms and accommodatory mechanisms. But of what is this equilibrium composed?

First it is noted that the purest accommodation is oriented activity—"a choice," says Piaget—which comes only after an assimilation has clashed with the unforeseen of the environmental reality. Stressing the active and sometimes "initiatory" character of accommodation, Piaget emphasizes that ". . . accommodation is always relative to assimilation because a subject would not accommodate to a given reality if he were not trying to assimilate that same reality" (Piaget, 1958, *Lecture de l'experience*, p. 65). Therefore, there is accommodation only if there has been an attempted or tentative assimilation, the failure of which incites the accommodatory adjustments: "It is the effort to extend the coordination of schemes, not an immediate tendency for accommodation itself, that causes the subject to become interested in differences in reality" (Piaget, 1936, p. 418).

Assimilation, which is the origin of schemes, is basic to the development of cognition, but it is "deforming" if it is not counterbalanced by accommodation; such deformation is noted in the early stages of development and in symbolic play because in these instances the child does not yet possess the logical framework which allows him to integrate the findings derived from experience. *A progressive equilibration* with accommodation which accompanies the development of operations allows assimilation to become "preserving" (in contrast to the "deforming" *assimilation* of the preceding level).*

Working Hypotheses

Within this general Piagetian framework, the present study seeks to examine the effect of blindness upon the development of the cognitive processes.

We have noted the emphasis accorded by Piaget to the role of operativity: i.e., the coordination of actions carried out by the subject on the objects in the assignment of significations. Also, it has been noted that the figurative structures play only a secondary role, a role of "container" or symbolic "signifier."

Blindness can be characterized by a damage to the figurative structures. Deprivation of sight and accompanying difficulties of imitation bring, as we have underlined, an impoverishment, quantitative as well as qualitative, of perceptions and of their figurative representation.

However, there is an important point: the perceptual deficiency of the blind is a *general and undifferentiated deficiency*: i.e., it does not pick out and center on any one perceptive aspect of objects. Our research differ profoundly from those of Bruner (1964). In his experiments, Bruner hid distorting perceptual cues, cues which the child must disregard: e.g., difference of water level in conservation of liquids. In the present study all perceptual cues, whether they favor the logical operation or not, are accessible visually for the sighted as well as tactually for the blind. Blindness tends to constitute an obstacle in the immediate organization of perceptions as well as a general limitation in the child's contact with outside objects.

The nature of the perceptual knowledge of blind subjects will be examined. For optimum development, tactilo-kinesthetic perception must be continuously employed; sweeping movements of the receptors serve as reactivators. Because the tactual perceptual field becomes dulled readily, constant exploratory movements are necessary for its reactivation; exploratory movements are indispensable and in this respect perceptual activity is in fact hard to dissociate from sensory motor activity.

The deprivation of sight makes it necessary for an individual to use exploratory tactilo-kinesthetic perceptions; this, in turn, requires increased activity. We shall eventually determine if such is the case with blind children.

---

*The emphasis accorded to assimilation in Piaget's later theoretical writings has caused apprehension among certain psychologists who fear that any work which suggests that knowledge originated from within the subject will promote a return to idealism. An article by Galifret–Granjon (1962) furnishes commentary on this aspect of Piaget's position.

There is note, however, that Piaget holds that *it is the activity of the subject which is the origin of operations and not the perceptions as such.* At this level it would seem that the operatory potential of the blind child is intact.

Also, the deprivation of sight does not affect the acquisition and utilization of language as a symbolic instrument and as a means of communication.

We see, then, why the study of blind children is important. Although blindness is characterized by a marked damage of the figurative structures, it is followed by normal language development. What effect do these conditions have on the development of logical operations? What effect do irregularities in figurative elements — i.e., perceptions and mental imagery — have in the constitution of the logical structures?

General Hypothesis

The general hypothesis is: *Genetically, there is a relationship between adequacy of materials on which operations are based and the development of these operations themselves.*

Two types of materials are considered "signifiers," which according to Piaget are: figurative elements — i.e., perception and mental imagery — which form the basis for concrete operations which involve manipulable objects; and structures of language which form the basis for verbal operations.

Our hypothesis implies that the existence of rich and differentiated figurative structures promotes the appearance of operations which depend on them, while an impoverishment of these structures will slow down the acquisition of these operations. Likewise, verbal operations would also depend in part on the degree of development attained by language.

Blindness is characterized by a diminution of environmental (perceptual) stimulation and a corresponding diminution of figurative representations. (The present reference is to a *diminution* and not a *suppression*, since the blind subject does possess other images: e.g., tactual, auditory.) While the figurative structures of the sighted are incomparably richer than the ones of the blind of the same age, there is no noticeable difference between these two groups in the language area.

The present study seeks to assess the effect of blindness on a third area, the development of logical operations.

Specific Hypotheses

Performance of the sighted will be significantly superior to that of the congenitally blind in operations which are based on figurative structures.

Because the figurative support is of greater importance in infralogical operations, performance of the congenitally blind will be significantly poorer in this area than in the area of logico-mathematical operations. In fact we have seen (pp. 00–00) that by reason of the relative approximation of images to the objects in cases of infralogical operations, the relations between the figurative and operative aspects are much more restricted than in the case of logico-mathematical operations.

Within the framework of logico-mathematical operations, the congenitally blind will behave differently in tasks based on actual manipulation of solid objects (which establishes a certain figurative support) from the way they behave in tasks where such figurative support is virtually nul, that is, in tasks which are based almost exclusively on verbal activities. The third hypothesis can be formulated as follows:

1. A systematic and significant inferiority of performance will be evidenced by the congenitally blind on measures of logical operations which involve concrete manipulation of perceptual material;

2. The performance of the congenitally blind will not differ significantly from that of the sighted on measures of logical operations which involve verbal content or oral presentation.

These hypotheses imply that when pathological factors (visual defects, in the circumstances), are present dissociation is possible in the development and in the appearance of different types of operations. This independence is relative and manifests itself in a sizeable deficiency in the infralogical sector, in that of concrete manipulations, and in a normal or quasi-normal development of the verbal logic sector. This introduces the problem of language and its relationships to operations. In our conclusions we shall discuss this in terms of the experimental results obtained.

Our last specific hypothesis relates to the degree of perceptive impoverishment caused by blindness. Studies previously cited have made clear that sensory restriction following infant blindness is more greater than that following blindness incurred later. The effects described above are more marked in the congenitally blind than for the adventitiously blind. In other words, we expect that:

1. Performance of the congenitally blind will be systematically inferior to that of the adventitiously blind in operations having a strong figurative support.

2. On the other hand, performance of the congenitally blind and of the adventitously blind will not differ in verbally based operations.

Limitations of the Study

Present comparison of blind and sighted children will be limited to the period of *concrete operations*: i.e., subjects will be between the ages of four or five and 10 or 11 years, a period during which concrete operations generally are achieved. The problems and the hypotheses can obviously have a wider scope, it seemed to us that a study provisionally confined within such limits could still lead to certain results, for two reasons:

1. At its initiation, the period of concrete operations is characterized by an "excessive" preponderance of perceptions and mental imagery which serve as an obstacle to operatory thought (Piaget, 1960). For this reason, the appearance of the first operatory behavior in the blind child for whom the figurative aspect is reduced is particularly interesting.

2. At the concrete level demarcation between infralogical and logico-mathe-matical operations has the greatest significance, while one of the main character-istics of the formal or hypothetico-deductive level is the ability to reason abstractly: i.e., without regard to possible concrete and spatial structures. Therefore, the role played by the perceptual aspects of objects is more ap-propriately assessed at a concrete level than at a formal one. Methodologically, it seemed appropriate to study a period where maximum effects are expected.

Additional studies which assess the development of formal thought in blind and in sighted adolescents are required to determine if findings from the present work can be generalized.

Part Two

EXPERIMENTAL RESEARCH: The Formation of the Reasoning Process in Blind Children

Chapter Three

METHODOLOGY

Experimental Design

Theoretical Basis for Experiments

The different experiments have theoretical ties, and are directly derived from our hypotheses. Tasks have been selected which involve both infralogical operations (spatial and physical) and logical operations. Infralogical operations are those which tend to the construction of the object itself (space, time, etc.), while logical operations establish ties *between* objects (classifications, seriations, numbers). The former deal with the different parts of the object, and are based on relationships involving position, displacement, division into parts, etc., while the latter apply to comparative relations: e.g., likeness or difference between distinct objects.

Within logical operations (classifications and seriations) there is distinction between those which involve figurative support (e.g., concrete material manipulation), and the ones in which the figurative support is reduced or non-existent: i.e., essentially based on verbal support.

In fact there is a perfectly forseeable problem. In effect, the present study is limited to the period of concrete operations, a period which reaches completion around nine to 11 years of age. It may seem contradictory to look for purely verbal tasks which rely on concrete support since, by definition, operations at the "concrete level" are characterized by their exclusive application to material realities. Yet, after much exploration, we were able to study certain forms of logical reasoning based almost exclusively on verbal statements, which are concrete rather than formal operations, and therefore remain comparable to the logical operations that are based on manipulation of objects.

Technical Contingencies

Although our theoretical bases are relatively clear, certain practical and technical problems have caused our research to follow a certain direction. Three points relative to the adaptation of tests to blindness and tactual perceptive prehension must be emphasized:

1. Effort must be made to avoid interference with academic achievement. Blind children generally are two or three grade levels behind sighted children. Therefore, comparison of the two groups in areas such as number concepts was omitted because of this difficulty.

2. Because interest is in conceptual rather than motor ability, and in order to eliminate bias, tasks were chosen in which successful performance was not unduly influenced by manual dexterity. When necessary, the child was reminded of an object which was on the table outside of his perceptual field, and he was assisted in placing objects where he wanted them.

3. In order to keep things simple, the specific verbal instructions which accompany each experiment are not listed here, but at the initiation of each task the child was encouraged to explore the proposed material at length; responses were not accepted until this had occurred completely, a fact that could be as certained by observing the child's gestures.

Sampling

The Blind

Definition of blindness

For the purposes of this study the blind are defined as subjects who are totally deprived of useful vision (zero vision), or who have only light perception. Any other definition, legal or scientific, is not accepted.

1. *Congenital blindness*: The congenitally blind (CB) are those subjects who were diagnosed blind either *at birth* or during the first year of life.

2. *Adventitious blindness*: The adventitiously blind (AB) are those subjects who became blind *after the age of four years*: i.e., subjects whose early development was normal or quasi-normal. Note, however, that this group includes a certain number of subjects who experienced progressive impairment prior to age four although they did not totally lose their sight until after that age. One type classified under this category is the congenitally "amblyopic" children who progressively reach total blindness.

Because of the low incidence of adventitious blindness, amblyopic subjects are included in the sample of the adventitiously blind which, while not always a desirable practice, seems legitimate in this case. A superiority of the adventitiously blind over the congenitally blind is hypothesized; therefore, the early visual deficiency of some of the adventitiously blind in our group should serve to decrease these differences. If significant differences between the two groups, which favor the adventitious group, are found, they will serve to emphasize our position.

Selection criteria

Subjects who had handicaps other than blindness, handicaps which might impair their performance or cast doubt on the psychological interpretation, were not included in the study. Selection criteria were:

1. *Normal verbal IQ*: Only those having a verbal IQ of 80 or above, as measured by the Interim Hayes–Binet Test or the WISC Verbal Scale, were included.

A serious question arises at this point. What is the necessity or meaning of this criterion? In raising this question at the outset, do we not risk influencing the final results? The following points, however, serve to justify selection solely on the basis of verbal IQ:

a. Hayes has shown, and our Paris work has confirmed, that the incidence of mental retardation is greater in the visually handicapped than in the normally sighted. This increased incidence of retardation among the blind means only that multiple handicaps frequently are observed within the same subject. Although the two may have a common etiology, it should not be assumed that one of the handicaps causes the other. Nevertheless, a random sample of blind subjects contains approximately five times as many mentally retarded as a random sample of sighted subjects (10% vs. 2%). Any comparison between blind and sighted should acknowledge this fact.

b. In a sample drawn from public primary school classes one is in fact guaranteed that subjects are of approximately normal intellectual ability because mentally retarded students have been removed from the regular classes into special classes. However, such classes do not exist for blind retarded children in the Paris area. Instead, these multiply-handicapped children are placed in classes or institutions for the blind. Therefore, it is necessary to select the blind sample on the basis of IQ.

c. Finally, we must consider a possible objection that sample bias could occur if subjects are originally selected on the basis of verbal IQ. In other words, if our hypotheses are confirmed and the operatory verbal level of the blind approximates that of the normal, this fact may be fully explained by the pre-selection. But analysis of the contents of the Interim Hayes–Binet Test and the Wechsler Intelligence Scale for Children (WISC) Verbal Test indicates this should not cause bias. Both tests are composed of a variety of components: e.g., vocabulary, short-term memory, comprehension, absurd sentences, similarities, etc. Hayes (Levine, 1950) found a certain inferiority among the blind on "logical" tasks (e.g., similarities, absurd sentences, etc.), whereas better performance was noted on tasks involving vocabulary and short-term memory. Consequently blind persons with an average verbal IQ frequently have above average performance on tasks which do not require logical reasoning.

To emphasize this point, let us distinguish between both the Interim Hayes–Binet and the WISC Verbal Tests, the tasks which assess mainly "logical"processes from those which assess more "automatic" processes (e.g., vocabulary, general information, memory). The Hayes–Binet contains 30 items between the age levels of six to 10 (5 age levels × 6 items per level); out of these, 12 are "logical" items, 18 "automatic," or, in percentages 40 versus 60 percent. In the WISC Verbal Test, the percentages are 33 and 66 percent respectively.

In both tests, items which involve logical reasoning make only minor contributions to the determination of the verbal IQ. Also, we know the blind perform less well on items involving sight. Therefore, we are put in an unfavorable position in relation to our hypotheses, which postulate normal or nearly normal behavior on the part of the blind during verbal logical tests.

These reasons appear to justify selection of our blind subjects on the basis of individual verbal IQ. Note, however, that there is not a hypothesized relationship between the mental age (or IQ) and the operatory level; to assume such a relationship is not the object of the study.

2. There must be an *absence of any other physical handicaps:* e.g., deafness or auditory impairment, effects of poliomyelitis, brain damage, encephalitis, hemiplegia, etc.

3. Subjects must have had *regular school attendance.*

4. *School level*: Blind subjects under nine years of age must be functioning at a grade level not more than two years below that expected for normals of equivalent age. Blind subjects over nine years of age must be functioning at a grade level not more than three years below that expected for normals of equivalent age. Here it is remembered that the academic performance of blind students generally is two to three years below that of sighted students of equivalent age.

Etiology of blindness

Etiology of the experimental group of blind subjects varies, but essentially includes: retrolental fibroplasia (RLF), glaucoma, congenital malformations, glioma, retinitis pigmentosa, retinal detachment due to myopia, and physical injury which results in adventitious blindness.

Limited size of the sample does not permit us to examine the specific effects of the different etiologies on observed behavior. However, one category, RLF, is of particular interest. While practically non-existent today, this ocular affliction was relatively frequent between 1944 and 1955. It was caused by an excessive supply of oxygen in the early electric incubators which were developed to save premature babies. The excess oxygen caused a dehydration of the ocular tissues, and, consequently, a practically irreversible alteration of the retina. Although a more approximate ratio of oxygen and hydrogen in the incubators has reduced the danger of such accidents, RLF remains an important factor in our education institutions because these premature blind babies have now reached the school age.

The problem is, evidently, to determine if (1) the prematurity in itself could cause sub-normal mental development during infancy, or if (2) the alterations due to the excess of oxygen were localized at the peripheral ocular level, or, finally, if (3) there were concomitant injuries to other brain tissues.

These premature RF babies have been the subject of relatively extensive psychological and medical studies. In general, the findings indicate an ocular localization of the disorder which, generally, is not followed by mental deficiency.

This position is supported by conclusions derived from research by Norris, Spaulding, and Brodie (1957); their goal was to determine if the early intellectual development of blind premature infants differed from that of babies whose blindness was due to other causes. No significant difference was found.

Parmelee (1959) also states that while the intellectual development of the prematures is not inferior to that of other blind children, they tend to experience delays in physical development (size and weight) and to exhibit general nervous fragility and psychomotor difficulties. These, he believes, are related more to their prematurity than to their blindness per se.

Nonetheless, there was effort to control a possible relationship between RLF, prematurity, and lowered intellectual ability. The experimental groups contain only those blind subjects, some of whom were RF, whose IQ was 80 or above, thus eliminating prematures who were mentally retarded. Furthermore, where it was feasible, the performance of RF children was compared with that of children whose blindness had other causes. As will be noted later, no significant differences were found between the performances of these two groups.

Sex of subjects

There was effort to equate groups in terms of sex. All experimental groups were randomly drawn. Males comprised 50 percent to 60 percent of the various sub-groups. In previous studies, sex was not found to be a significant variable.

Adverse social influences

Because of the low incidence of blindness in France, educational institutions for the blind are boarding schools where some children may come from remote rural areas and others from urban sectors. In fact, the two educational institutions in the Paris area from which subjects were drawn (Institut National des Jeunes Aveugles, at Paris, and Institut Departemental des Aveugles de la Seine, at Saint-Mandé) handle approximately 25 percent of the total blind population of the French schools. About 60 percent of these children were originally drawn from rural areas. On the other hand, the sighted control groups were drawn from the public elementary schools of Paris and generally came from an urban environment. Because of these original differences in locale, approximately 50 percent of the blind sample was living away from home, while all the members of the sighted control group were living at home.

Finally, there were other disrupting factors in the lives of the blind subjects. The family's shock and reaction to a disabled child, the parents' lack of knowledge about causal factors and about recommended training procedures quite often engender a *familial overprotection*. In turn, the overprotection makes it even more difficult for the child to learn, since it contributes to the formation of anxiety reactions, insecurity, and affective and social dependency.

Duration of study

The different experiments described in the following chapters were in groups of two or three over a period of four school years, beginning with the fall of 1959 and extending to the summer of 1963.

Because of this time interval, the experimental subjects are not identical in all the experiments. Turnover of subjects was approximately 10 percent a year (new students, children who were previously too young becoming eligible, withdrawals, etc.). Over the four-year period approximately 30 blind children in the experimental group passed all the tasks at different time intervals.

The Sighted

Selection of the sighted (control group) did not involve the problems which were encountered in the selection of the blind sample.

Selection criteria

All sighted subjects were drawn from kindergarten and elementary grades of public schools in the Paris area, and grade placement was that expected for their age. Students who had repeated a grade or who had accelerated promotion were not included.

As in the blind group, only one or two tests were administered to a given subject and different groups were formed for each new wave of experiments.

Work of the sighted in tactual perception

In certain cases, the sighted were further divided into two sub-groups. One group used sight and worked in the usual manner; the other group worked under conditions similar to those experienced by the blind: i.e., the material was completely hidden behind a screen and could only be explored tactually. The latter group will be termed ST (sighted-tactual perception) while the former will be called SV (sighted-visual perception).

The comparison between these groups—SV, ST, and CB (congenitally blind)—will be of particular interest because the ST subjects, although temporarily deprived of their sight, have the benefit of previous experience in this domain. In the study they are in a situation intermediate to that of the SV, the sighted who can use all their sensory organs, and the situation of the CB, the blind totally deprived of visual representations.

Grouping in Terms of Age

For the blind, as for the sighted, age range of subjects within each age group is 11 months; i.e., children with CA 8 range from CA 8-0 to CA 8-11, etc. Therefore, the mean age of this group is approximately eight years six months, although they are referred to as CA 8, for simplicity's sake.

Statistical Analysis of Findings

Use of Non-Parametric Statistics

Congenital blindness is rare in France, as noted already. Because of the selection criteria described above, the experimental groups of blind subjects were limited in numbers. Only 10 to 20 subjects of each age level were available in Paris.

It is evident that under these conditions, certain statistical techniques are of dubious value not only because they require larger groups, but they are based on normal distributions. Futhermore, it was never possible for us to test the normality of the distribution of such small groups, nor the homogeneity of variance of the blind and sighted groups. For these reasons we preferred to use non-parametric tests which offer the twofold advantage of requiring only small groups and of hypothesizing neither normality nor homogenity of variance.

Because all the tests were not given to a subject during one session it was not possible to pool test results or individual test profiles for comparison. Instead, there will be a report on each experiment.

Comparison between Groups

Comparison Blind/Sighted, SV or ST

Comparison will be made of the various independent groups within the same age group; these independent groups were subjected to the same selection criteria.

Comparison of Congenitally Blind and Adventitiously Blind

Because of the low incidence of adventitiously blind compared to the congenitally blind, once those with concomitant handicaps were eliminated (brain tumors, meningitis, etc.), it was not possible to maintain the previously described age groups for subjects in this category. To make comparison possible, however, groups were formed of AB subjects of different age ranges, and these were carefully *matched* with corresponding groups of CB subjects as later described.

The matching was essentially based on chronological age, mental age, and school level. If differences existed, the congenitally blind group generally was the one with a slight advance in age. Therefore, any discrepancies in the performance of CB subjects cannot be attributed to slight biases in terms of mental or chronological age.

Chapter Four

INFRALOGICAL OPERATIONS I: Spatial Representation and Displacement

According to Piaget, spatial—infralogical—operations function in a manner parallel to logico-mathematical operations that start from given objects in order to bring them together. In spatial infralogical operations the similarities between objects, which characterize classificatory logical operations, are replaced by those of proximity and separation; notions of disparity which are basic to seriations are replaced by those of order and placement. Finally, the notions of number, which evolve from sets and correspondence, are replaced by those of measure.

The spatial operations which we are about to study are the operations of order, or, to be more exact, the change of order which characterizes *displacement*.

At the sensory-motor level, the 18-month-old child is already able to coordinate his own displacements into an integrated reversible system which allows him to direct himself without difficulty in familiar surroundings ("grouping of displacements"). In the same fashion, he learns to recognize objects from different perspectives, and to organize these varying perspectives into a coherent structure. Thus, the infant soon learns to recognize his bottle regardless of its position in space and to turn it around to take hold of the nipple.

Although the displacements of his own body and displacement of objects are coordinated at the sensory-motor stage in a rather precocious way, this is not true of coordination at the representational level. A longer period of maturation is required before the child is able to translate mentally sensory-motor spatial acquisitions. Thus, he will be seven or eight years old before he will be able to draw the route he takes every day to school or to reproduce the plan of his bedroom. Similarly, it is not until seven or eight that he becomes capable of imagining the displacement of an object and the different locations it is going to occupy in that process.

To illustrate this, two experiments will be described which involve displacement of objects.

For correct anticipation of the positions of a moving object, the different parts of the object must remain in the same relative position. Then it is necessary to coordinate these relations with the direction of the course followed by the object.

But until the child attains a certain operatory level, his forecasts are false because his perception of the object at the starting point is merely transposed to the final, or arrival, point.

Comparison will be made of the appearance of this type of operation in blind and sighted children.

Two-Dimensional Displacement

The following experiment took place during the 1961 to 1962 school year at the Centre International d'Epistemologie Genetique of Geneva. Detailed description of the technique used and of the obtained results are the subject of a separate publication (Hatwell, 1964). Therefore, only pertinent aspects of the study are reviewed now.

Description and Material

The material evolved from a study which Inhelder termed "Le tour du lac" ("Around the Lake"), and from research by Taponnier on the concept of "between." In it, the child is asked to suppose a composite object formed of three elements—A, B, and C—moving along a closed course; the child then forecasts the position of the different elements of the object at diverse locations on the course. *The problem involves the anticipation of the positions of different parts of an object during a displacement or movement of the object in a given direction.*

The material consists of a wooden board of unusual shape (an irregular eight-sided polygon) on which three wooden rails have been attached in a concentric

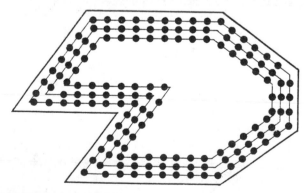

Fig. 1 Wooden polygon with three attached rails parallel to edge of board based on Inhelder's "Around the Lake"

order and parallel to the edge of the board (Fig. 1). These rails have a series of holes in their top surface, spaced in such a way that the holes of the three rails form a straight line at any point of the course. The child is told the board is "an island" which has three "rails" running along the shore. The eight sides of the polygon are labelled S1, S2, S3, etc.

On the side there is a number of steel pins ¼" in length, with three different types of head: balls, cubes, and cylinders.* The fit of the pins into the holes in the rails is secure enough to permit tactual exploration (Fig. 2). These pins represent the "cars" of a train travelling on the rails around the board.

Fig. 2 Cylinders, balls & cubes—different heads of pins used in rails.

Technique

Situation I: Cars in Line

1. *Case 1: Spontaneous Answers*: A "train" of three pins (one cylinder, one ball, one cube)—A, B, C—is placed at the "station" on S1 (side one) on the inside rail of the board. The child is asked to anticipate the position it will occupy when arriving at Station S3, after moving clockwise along the rails. To answer, the child has three separate pins identical to those of the model-train, which he will have to locate in sequence at S3 "as if it was this train (the model-train) which has arrived there."

When a solution is given by the child the pins are removed from S3, and the train continues on its "trip," and will stop successively at S4, S5, S6, S7, and S8. If the child succeeds in forecasting all the positions, the examiner proceeds to Situation II. If the child fails to forecast any of the positions, the examiner presents Case 2.

2. *Case 2: Game Involving Demonstration and Evidence*: The "answer-train" (the three pins which were supplied the child) remains at S8 as the subject's attention is directed back to the model-train which is still in the station at S1. It is explained to the child that the cylinder (or "the steam-roller) is the car which always moves first, because it is the engine which pulls the other cars and these are always behind it." The child then follows the course with his finger, and notes his mistake: "Now you put the cube ahead. You changed the engine. You haven't the right to do that." The trip is started over again, and the train stops first at S2. If the child gives the correct answer for S2, he is asked to stop successively at S3, S4, etc. If his answer is still incorrect, the demonstration is repeated again.

---

*Blind children of the age included in the present study have acquired tactual discrimination of these three forms.

In this instance the three answer-pins are left at S2, as the train successively goes to S3, S4, S5, S6, S7, and S8. At each stop, the child is given an additional set of three pins, while the previous sets remain at the stations already reached. At the end of the game, eight sets of pins are on the board at the successive positions S1 through S8.

The above technique was devised in order to facilitate finding the solution; awareness of spatial proximity of the stations helps the child, as does tactual verification of positions.

Situation II: Parallel Cars

In this situation the cars are not placed in line on one rail; instead they are placed parallel, each car on one of the three rails lining the edge. After stating that "no-one can ever switch rails because it would mean a serious accident," the experiment proceeds in the same manner as Situation I.

1. *Case 1: Spontaneous Answers*: Successive stops at the stations S3, S4, S5, S6, S7, and S8.

2. *Case 2: Game of Demonstration and Evidence*: Examiner demonstrates the child's mistake by having the child's finger follow the rail and find "that the cube took the place of the steam-roller." The same technique is used as in Situation I, each set of answer-pins staying in place at each station as the cars move around the board.

Note: As mentioned in the preceding chapter, precautions were taken to assure that subjects employing tactual perception were completely familiar with the material prior to the initiation of the task. They were told to follow with their fingers the presumed course of the train from the starting station to the stop involved in that phase of the problem. If necessary, they were provided assistance in inserting the pins in the holes of the rails which they had chosen. Thus, insufficiencies due to possible motor difficulties did not interfere with test performance.

Sample

Table 1 sets forth the number of SV subjects (sighted who employed visual perception), of ST subjects (sighted who employed tactual perception as objects were explored from behind a screen), and CB subjects (congenitally blind) included in the present study.

Table 1
Number of SV subjects (sighted, visual perception), ST subjects
(sighted, tactual perception), and CB subjects (congenitally blind)

CA	5	6	7	8–9	10	11
SV	15	15	19			
ST			15			
CB				12	13	11

Admittedly, the groups compared—SV, ST, and CB—are not of equivalent age. The ages at which the behaviors being studied become operational vary from group to group.

Results

Note: The sequence of the cars in the train is A–B–C, and this sequence must be maintained at all locations, S1 through S8. Three scores are possible: (1) *total failure*: the order C–B–A is always forecast; (2) *partial success*: sometimes the order A–B–C, sometimes the order C–B–A, is forecast; (3) *total success*: the order A–B–C is forecast in all the positions.

Situation I: Cars in Line

The percentages of total successes and partial successes have been determined for Case 1 (spontaneous answers) and for Case 2 (after-the-demonstration game). Figures 3 and 4 summarize the results.

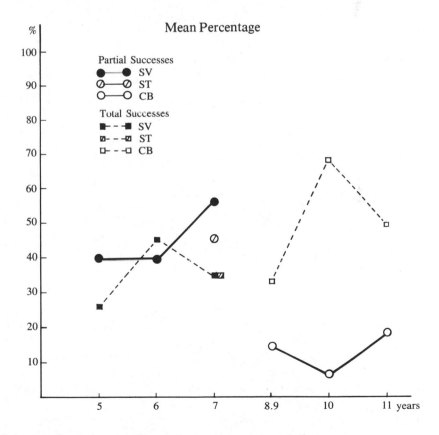

Fig. 3 Percentages of total successes and partial successes. Situation 1, Case 1 (spontaneous answers)

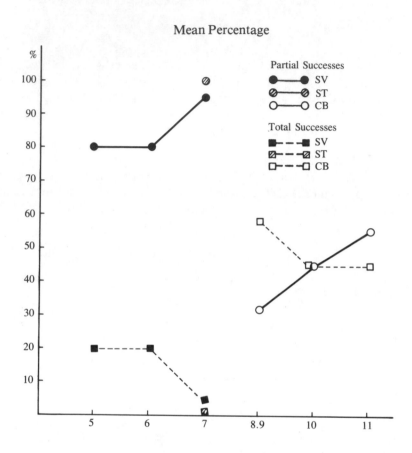

Fig. 4 Percentages of total successes and partial successes.
Situation 1, Case 2 (demonstration and evidence game)

1. When compared with the sighted who employ visual perceptions, the congenitally blind show a retardation of approximately six years. In terms of total success, the performance of the congenitally blind, CA-11, is significantly inferior to that of the sighted, SV, CA-5. Moreover, the decalage is maintained even after Case 2 provides demonstration and participation in the evidence game.

2. The curves representing the distribution of successes among the blind and the sighted are parallel.

3. The ST subjects (sighted who employ tactual perception as objects are explored from behind a screen) have performance equivalent to that of sighted subjects of the same age who employ visual perception (SV).

Situation II: Parallel Cars

Figures 5 and 6 show the percentages of total and partial successes for each of the three groups.

Mean Percentage

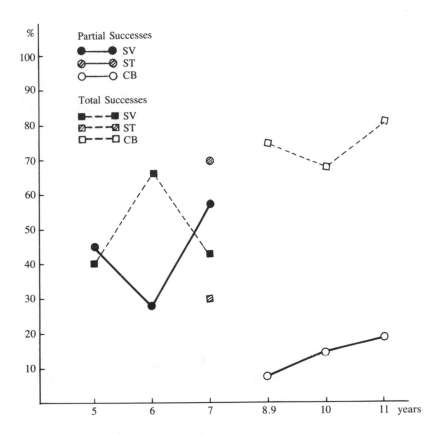

Fig. 5 Percentages of total successes and partial successes.
Situation 2, Case 1 (spontaneous answers)

Again, the less successful performance of the blind is equivalent to that observed in Situation I: i.e., at CA–11 performance of the CB approximates that of the SV, CA–5. This is true in Case 1 (spontaneous answers) as well as in Case 2 (demonstration and evidence game). Too, there again is no significant difference between SV and ST subjects of the same CA.

Mean Percentage

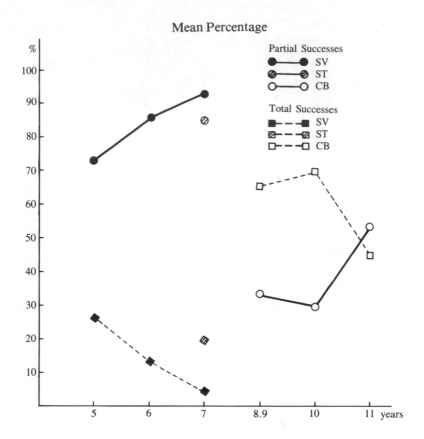

Fig. 6 Percentage of total successes and partial successes.
Situation 2, Case 2 (demonstration and evidence game)

Comparison Between Congenitally Blind (CB) and Adventitiously Blind (AB)

To verify our hypothesis that early blindness is a much more serious handicap than late blindness, a group of eight adventitiously blind children, ages eight to 11, was administered this test. Their performances were compared with those of a group of eight congenitally blind which was randomly selected from the general sample. The two groups, adventitiously and congenitally blind, were matched as closely as possible in terms of chronological age, mental level, and school level. In Situation I, differences between CB and AB which favored the AB were significant at a .005 level. Similarly, in Situation II differences between the two groups were at the same level of significance (Fisher Test).

Our two hypotheses seemed to be confirmed in this experiment. The congenitally blind group was inferior to the sighted group, and also significantly inferior to the group of adventitiously blind.

Because of the importance of the deficit observed, a double check seemed appropriate. First, there was desire to verify the homogeneity of the congenitally blind group. Earlier mention was made (page   ) of the problems created by the etiology of blindness and particularly by RF and its associated prematurity. Indeed, approximately 45 percent of our subjects had been premature infants. Is their performance difficulty due to blindness, as such, or is it one of the after-effects of the overoxygenation which caused the atrophy of retinal cells? This is the first control we shall establish. Secondly, is the assessment material too complicated, too "abstract"? Are the rules and instructions, particularly those concerning the symbolic aspect of the game, understood by the blind subjects? Even though the examiner always took steps to insure that both blind and sighted subjects understood the problem perfectly, and that they conformed to the experimental situation, the experiment was repeated with a material which was simpler and more familiar to the child. This second control will verify the results obtained.

Controls

Comparison of Retrolental Fibroplasia (RF) Subjects and Blind Subjects with Other Etiologies

From the total group of congenitally blind, the 17 subjects aged seven to 11 whose cause of blindness was retrolental fibroplasia, were matched with 17 congenitally blind subjects whose blindness was of another origin. Significant differences were not obtained between the two groups (Fisher Test) in either Situation I or Situation II.

Control experiments

Except for simplified materials the assessment techniques were those used in Situation I of the main experiment.

1. *"Train" experiment* — Materials for the experiment included plastic rails forming a circular track of 20 inches in diameter, and two identical plastic trains composed of an engine, a freight car, and a flat car. At the opening of the experiment Train-1 was placed at location "S" ("the station"), and the child was asked to predict the position of the engine and of the two cars when the train arrived at the location directly across from "S." During this time Train-1 did not move from "S." The child answered by placing Train-2 on the rails "as if it were Train-1 (the one at the station) which had stopped here for a little while."

The test was administered to congenitally blind subjects, ages eight, nine, 10, and 11 years, and also to sighted subjects SV (visual perception), ages four and five years. Although the differences were greater they confirmed those previously obtained. Indeed, the test was "easier" for the sighted who previously had successful performance at five years of age, whereas the number of successes among the blind was the same as in the main experiment. The finding indicates that concrete and familiar material facilitates performance of the sighted only, and in doing so accentuates the differences between them and the blind.

2. *"Highway" experiment*—On an "S" shaped metallic highway (Fig. 7), a toy truck was placed at starting point "M." The child was then provided a second toy truck, identical to the first one, and was asked to place it at locations P, Q, and R successively, "as if it were this truck (the one motionless in M) that had arrived here (P, Q, or R) and had to stop for a red traffic light."

The second part of the experiment was the same as the first except that the truck was replaced by a plastic dog. In the third part, both the truck and the dog were used, and the following story was related: "The truck was going slowly (from M to N) because it was carrying big chunks of meat; the dog was *running behind* it, trying to steal a chunk of meat; they both have to stop (successively) at P, Q, and R for traffic lights." The child must predict the respective positions of the truck and the dog at these different points along the course.

The goal of this experiment is to analyze the blind subjects' comprehension of the notions "before-behind" (in space), "before-behind" (in time), etc., in relation to a given object and in function of a given displacement. The obtained results substantiate those observed earlier: performance of blind subjects, ages 10 and 11, continued to be inferior to that of the five-year-old SV sighted subjects who employed visual perception.

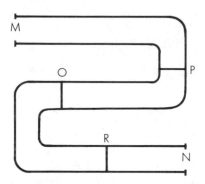

Fig. 7 S-shaped metallic highway used in experiment to analyze notion of "ahead-behind" and "before-behind"

Summary and Conclusions

The congenitally blind show serious retardation when compared to the sighted subjects, regardless of whether the sighted employ visual perception or tactual perception. The data also demonstrate that the adventitiously blind are significantly superior to the congenitally blind.

As these results confirm our hypothesis, they also confirm previous indications of the difficulties encountered by the blind in spatial imagery. Prior to detailed discussion of this point a report will be given on the results of a second experiment in which the displacement is three- rather than two-dimensional.

Rotation Around an Axis

As in the preceding experiment, the problem is to forecast the position of different parts of a composite object as it moves along a predetermined course. The difference is that the displacement no longer involves a two-dimensional situation (the plane); instead it is in a three-dimensional one: an object revolves a full 180° around one of its axes. Actually, this experiment is just a complicated version of the preceding one.

Material

The basic equipment is a metallic frame formed by three vertical and four horizontal bars which divide it into six compartments or "squares" (Fig. 8). A small object is attached to each compartment: e.g., toy car, a wooden circle, a key, a cube, a cup from a doll's tea set, and a cylindrical bead.

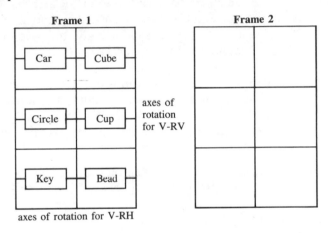

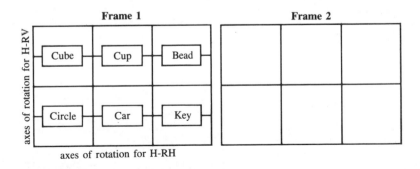

Fig. 8 Metallic frames with six compartments.

In addition, there is a second frame, identical to the first one, except that the compartments are empty. Also, there are six objects; the objects are identical to those attached inside the compartments of the first frame. These objects are not tied to the frame and are given to the child outside it.

Technique

The two frames are placed flat on the table. The bar on the right side of the frame we shall call "vertical" for purposes of clarity. The vertical bar on the right side of the frame remains flat against the table. Frame 1 is rotated around its axis. When the frame arrives in a position perpendicular to the surface of the table the child is asked to imagine the second half of the rotation and to place the objects inside the empty frame "as if this one (Frame 1) had been completely turned around on the table."

If the subject fails, the rotation of Frame 1 is completed, and the subject checks his mistakes. The examiner then proceeds to the second rotation: at the start, the frame is in a vertical position, then it is rotated around its lower "horizontal" bar. In case of failure, the second rotation is also followed by a demonstration. But in later failures no demonstration is given. Four forms of rotation were presented twice each, for a total of eight anticipations; order of appearance was altered in the second presentation. The forms of rotation were:

1. Frame in "vertical" position, rotation around a vertical axis: V–RV
2. Frame in "vertical" position, rotation around a horizontal axis: V–RH
3. Frame in "horizontal" position, rotation around a vertical axis: H–RV
4. Frame in "horizontal" position, rotation around a horizontal axis: H–RH.

Note: If, in working the problem, the child encountered difficulties—e.g., two objects placed in the same compartment, or an object left on the table, etc.—the examiner intervened.

Sample

The sample was composed of five groups:
Congenitally blind:
  a. 10 subjects, ages 8–9 years
  b. 12 subjects, age 10
  c. 10 subjects, age 11
Sighted SV (visual perception):
  d. 15 subjects, age 6
  e. 15 subjects, age 7

Results

Note: All six objects had to be placed in the correct compartments for the performance to receive a successful rating.

The percentage of successes (on all eight parts of the problem) for each of the SV and CB groups are summarized in Figure 9.

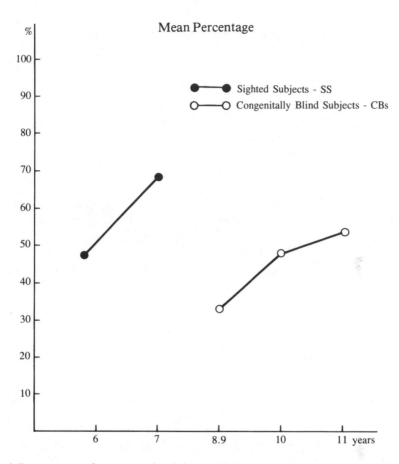

Fig. 9 Percentage of successes in eight predictions

Results clearly indicate that, when compared to the sighted, the blind experience a four-year delay. Performance of blind subjects, CA 10, approximates that of sighted subjects, CA 6. Differences between the sighted CA 6 and the blind CA 8–9 is significant at the .001 level (X^2 test).

Mistakes of the blind are variable. Of particular interest is the type of error in which consideration of displacement is neglected in predicting the invariance of positions. In this case, the subject reproduces (in the empty frame) the arrangement of the objects as he actually perceives it in the other frame with no regard for earlier explanations and demonstrations. When this behavior consistently appeared (e.g, among the very young) the subject was eliminated and it was noted that the the task was impossible for him to perform. Usually the error was temporary and reflected the child's difficulty in imagining the effects of the displacement.

Table 2 sets forth the frequency of a termed "answer without transformation" (i.e, answers in which all six objects were placed inside the empty frame without taking into consideration the announced rotation of the frame).

Table 2
Percentage of answers "without transformation"

CA	6	7	8–9	10	11
SV	19.6	6.3			
CB			8.3	13.9	20.8

Approximately 20 percent of the responses of the six-year-old sighted subjects was without transformation, whereas only 6.3 perent of the seven-year-old subjects responded in this manner. Differences which favored the seven-year-old groups were at the .005 level. By contrast, differences significant at the .05 level occurred between the performance of the eight- to nine-year-old group and the 11-year-old group of blind subjects. In this instance the older subjects demonstrated the poorer performance.

Although there was a diminution of other types of failures, the somewhat paradoxical error increase set forth in Table 2 demonstrates the difficulties encountered by the blind in the representation of moving objects. Because of their inability to imagine the result of such a displacement, the blind deny not only the transformation which involves the object, but also the resulting modifications in the spatial arrangement of its components.

These results were all the more surprising because, in his everyday life, the blind child has early exposure to similar situations. Indeed, the Braille graphic system is based on a reversal. Each letter can be enclosed in a theoretical cell composed of six points (three lines and two columns with a distance of approximately 2mm between them). The different combinations of these theoretical points constitute the entire Braille alphabet. But in writing Braille, the embossment is obtained by pricking the sheet with a sharp point. To read what he is writing, the child must then turn the sheet over. In other words, if Braille is read from *left* to right, like print, it is written from *right* to left. What is written is the mirror image of what is read (Fig. 10).

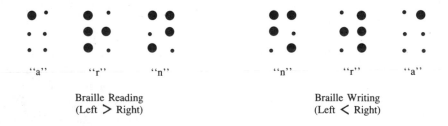

Braille Reading
(Left > Right)

Braille Writing
(Left < Right)

Fig. 10 Braille as read and braille as written.

The performances of the eight- to nine-year-old blind children are expected; few read Braille proficiently at this age, but the data indicate that difficulties of reversal persist at the 10- to 11-year level in blind children although nearly all of them can read material written either by hand or by machine. These difficulties are much greater than they are in sighted children of the same age. Behavior of the blind subjects during the experiment is interesting: very few of them recognized the similarity between this task and Braille hand-writing, although the V–RV position is just a large-scale reproduction of the arrangement of the Braille cell. Moreover, the few subjects who did realize the situations were similar did not necessarily succeed in forecasting the location of individual objects, even at the V–RV position.

But there is more to it than that. Some teachers of the blind believe it is preferable for the blind child to be unconscious of the reversal of writing in relationship to reading, and that, at the beginning of learning, it may be dangerous to apprise the child of that fact. The teaching is based on a principle of *automatization* of the movement, oriented from left to right when reading, and right to left when writing. The six theoretical points of the Braille letter are numbered from one to six, from the top to the bottom, and from the left to the right for reading; from the top to the bottom, and from the right to the left for writing. Consequently, each letter can be characterized by a "formula" which does not change. In the examples given in Figure 10, the letter "a" is composed by the point #1, the letter "n" by the points 1–3–4–5, the letter "r" by the points 1–2–3–5, both reading and writing.

Our observations indicate that knowledge of the Braille graphic system, which is, itself, based on reversal, does not help the blind in this experiment, and that they show on the contrary a four-year deficit in comparison with the sighted.

Summary and Discussion

The major findings which evolved from these two experiments are:

1. The congenitally blind show four to six years retardation, depending on the situation. At age 11, their performance is equivalent to that of five- to six-year-old subjects who work in visual perception;

2. The congenitally blind are significantly inferior to the adventitiously blind;

3. The development curves of the blind parallel those of the sighted: both move through the same sequence and experience the same type of error. There is a time-lag in the appearance of successes, but no difference in the quality or style of the behaviors;

4. Finally, the sighted whose work is behind a screen behave the same as the sighted of equivalent age who are allowed to use visual perception. For the ST group impoverishment of *actual* figurative elements does not exert a detrimental influence at the operative level. Success in such a task implies *earlier attainments* at the spatial level. This is experience the congenitally blind have not had.

The extensive deficit observed in these experiments confirms all previous findings concerning spatial representation in the congenitally blind. The originality of our experiments does not derive from verification of this established fact, but rather from the nuances which our studies have given it. At the response level we have tried to focus on the logical aspect of displacement and to eliminate, as much as possible, any perceptual motor or motor interference. Such interferences have caused difficulties in the interpretation of classical research in this field (Worchel, 1951; Drever, 1955; Hatwell, 1959).

To understand the nature of the difficulties encountered by the congenitally blind in tasks which require the anticipation of positions, we must consider the perceptual repercussions which blindness imposes on these subjects. The experiences of the blind, as well as the control they exert over these experiences, are inadequate; when objects of a certain size or moving at certain speeds are displaced, the blind control only the starting point, and, to a certain extent, the point of arrival (e.g., when a child looks for a toy he has thrown away, the displacement of his own body does not allow him to keep the spatial and proprioceptive cues he might have had, and he loses the left-right orientation of the objects in relation to himself). Therefore, when he perceives the position of the object at the end of the trajectory, it is very difficult for him to compare it with the one at the point of origin. Usually he does not know the intermediary positions of the moving object, and, in order to reconstruct them, he must start from the initially perceived position.

On the contrary, because of vision and the awareness which it permits, the sighted youth benefits from an infinity of "descriptive snapshots" of the object in motion or in transformation which will be progressively coordinated.

We can then understand that in the blind there is a tendency to anticipate a sameness in position in spite of an anticipated displacement; the final position is a *generalization of the position at the start*, which is the only perceived one, and which is the one that is maintained at the expense of another.

In conclusion, while our results confirm the advantages which accrue to the sighted child because of his multiple perceptions and his spatial-perceptual representations, it must be emphasized that the development curves of the blind closely parallel those of the sighted. What is observed in the blind is retarded acquisition, not a difference in the logical structuring or the mental elaboration of space. Although he achieves it at a later age, the congenitally blind child does achieve, within the framework of our experiments, logical organization of space similar to the one achieved by the sighted. From these findings it is inferred that similar results will be found in tasks which require other types of spatial operations. Thus, the controversy which was discussed in the review of the literature and which questioned the existence of a tactual space in the congenitally blind, and the equivalence of visual space in the sighted to tactual space of the blind, seems to be eliminated. Results indicate that spatial representation develops in spite of blindness, and that the nature of this structuring of space does not differ essentially from that achieved by the sighted. Visual deprivation only retards its construction, but the retardation is considerable and remnants of it remain after the congenitally blind reach adulthood.*

---

*Blind subjects often have difficulty with geometry. The difficulty stems not only from the handicap, but also from technical limitations in the presentation of the subject: there no an adequate process by which the blind student can correctly and easily draw the figures to which his reasoning applies.

Chapter Five

INFRALOGICAL OPERATIONS II: Physical Variations in Substance, Weight and Volume

Piaget's statement (Piaget and Inhelder, 1941, p. 243), "Invariance of thought is basic to logical reasoning," summarizes the primary importance he attaches to the progressive constitution of invariance, physical as well as logical, in the acquisition of knowledge.

Genetically, the first step in this progression is the development of a permanent object: by the end of his first year, the infant is able to recognize an object, i.e., to postulate its unity and identity through the multiple deformations which occur as it is perceived from various angles. He can also look for and "find back" an object which disappeared from his perceptual field, i.e., assert its independent and objective existence.

But object permanence, a characteristic acquisition of the sensory-motor stage, applies to the notion of a permanence only to a totally perceptible object. It does not yet apply to the parts of this object which, when brought together, constitute the total object. The permanence of objects does not as yet pertain to the real transformations which may transform it: division into parts, displacement of some parts in relation to others, reunification of divided parts, etc. Maturation is necessary to pass from the elementary form of invariance characterized by the permanent total object to the conservation of physical quantities which constitute the object itself, such as substance, weight, and volume. It is only between seven and 11 years that the child develops these notions, notions which are based on reversibility or the logical return to the earlier state (not the empirical and simple return which implies neither necessity nor deduction), and the composition of perceived differences (longer $\times$ thinner = bigger $\times$ shorter).

For Piaget, the main hindrance to physical composition and invariance is the perceptual appearance, i.e., the separate perceived relationships are considered as such and are not combined in rational systems integrating the successive states of the object and the steps in its transformation within a single mental construction.

The acquisition of the notion of conservation of quantities is divided into separate steps. Although the same logical scheme applies to the different concrete contents, a systematic order can be observed in the development of these notions of invariance: conservation of substance is achieved around seven years, weight around eight-to-nine years, and volume around 10-to-11 years. Piaget says that differences in age of achievement are due to the different perceptual modes required in the achievement of conservation of substance, weight and volume: the first (conservation of substance) relies on vision which confronts the individual with a universe of simultaneous data which is easy to structure and objectify, whereas the perceptual field of weighing is much narrower and requires a larger number of intellectual operations to coordinate the perceived relationships. Similar considerations apply to volume, coordination of these relationships being even more difficult than those in the handling of weight (Piaget and Inhelder, 1941, p. 241).

Is blindness (which creates a similarity between substance and weight as both are tactually apprehended) going to modify the discrepancy in ages which has always been observed in their acquisition? That is our first question. Blindness, furthermore, considerably reduces the quantity as well as the quality of the perceptual data reaching the subject. Since the blind are not as influenced as the sighted by "the immediate appearance of things", will the blind child understand the notion of invariance of physical quantities at an earlier age than the sighted child? Or, as already observed for spatial operations, will this perceptual deprivation slow down the appearance of operatory logical reasoning? The following experiment will attempt to answer these questions.

Description of Experiments

We have used the clay ball test, employing the technique developed at Geneva by Vinh Bang and communicated to us personally.

Conservation of Substance

The child compares two identical balls of modeling clay. After he has admitted their equality ("the same amount of dough"), he transforms one of the balls into a long thin sausage; then he is asked if there is still "as much dough in the ball as in the sausage or if there is more or less in the sausage, and why." The child again makes the sausage into a ball. He then transforms the ball into a flat "pancake". The examiner asks the same questions: "Does the pancake have the same amount, or more, or less dough than the ball?" The child makes the pancake back into a ball. He is then asked if the two balls are still the same. Next, the child divides one of the balls into four or five small pieces, and the examiner asks if there is more dough in the ball or more in the pieces or if there is the same amount in both.

Conservation of Weight

The method of assessment is the same as that followed in conservation of substance, except that the subject is asked if the sausage, pancake and odd pieces would *weigh* more than the ball. Scales are not used because most blind youths do not know how to use them. Instead, the subjects are asked to guess the weight.

Conservation of Volume

The usual technique consists of asking the child if the water level would rise the same amount when the sausage is immersed as it would when the ball is immersed. An important difficulty arose from the fact that a large number of blind children do not know, even those 10 or 11 years old, that level of the water rises, in a glass, when an object is placed in the water. When this lack of awareness becomes evident, the reason for the displacement is explained by saying that the "ball takes up room at the bottom of the glass, and moves out the water which has to rise."

Other portions of the experiment are the same as for substance and weight.

Order of Presentation

Sighted subjects: each group took only one test—either substance, weight or volume;

Congenitally blind subjects: because of the small number of blind subjects all those under twelve years of age started with conservation of substance, then took conservation of weight, and finally conservation of volume. Those over 12 years started with the conservation of weight, and if successful, proceeded to conservation of volume; if unsuccessful, they did conservation of substance instead.

Sample

Table 3 indicates the size of each age group taking the tests.

Table 3
Number of Sighted (SV) and Congenitally Blind (CB) Subjects
Administered Conservation of Substance, Weight, and Volume Assessments

CA		6	7	8	9	10	12-13	
Substance:	SV		20	18				
	CB	16		17	19	22	17	16
Weight	SV		20	21	32			
	CB	16		17	19	22	17	16
Volume:	SV					22		
	CB					22	17	16

Results

To be successful in the experiment, a subject had to affirm that there was conservation in all three transformations: sausage, pancake, and pieces: i.e., when he affirmed conservation of substance, weight or volume after the ball was transformed successively into a sausage, pancake, or little pieces. We shall compare these with cases of total non-conservation and partial conservation (Piaget's intermediate stages).

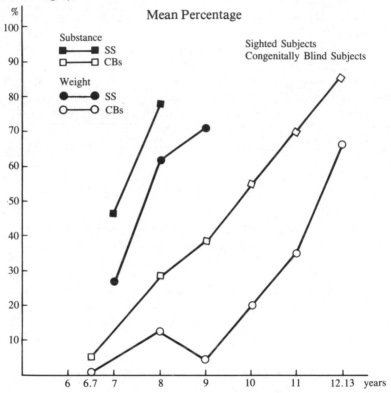

Fig. 11 Percentage of subjects by substance and by weight.

Conservation of Substance

Figure 11 sets forth the percentage of subjects of each age group who achieved conservation, as defined above. Blind subjects achieved conservation at a later age than sighted ones. When the chi-square test was employed with Yate's correction for small sample sized the differences between blind and sighted children, age eight, were significant at the .01 level, while differences between nine-year-old blind and eight-year-old sighted were significant at the .025 level. The performance of 10-year-old blind and eight-year-old sighted children did not differ statistically, nor did that of nine-year-old blind and seven-year-old sighted. In other words, when compared to sighted subjects the congenitally blind subjects showed an average delay of two years.

Conservation of Weight

The percentage of subjects in each age group who demonstrated conservation of weight, using the criterion established earlier, is presented in Figure 11. Difficulties encountered by the blind subjects again are apparent. Differences between blind subjects, age 10, and sighted children, age eight, are significant at the .01 level; although differences existed between the blind, age 11, and the sighted, age eight, they are not statistically significant (X^2).

Generally, blind subjects show a delay of approximately three years.

Conservation of Volume

Only one group of 22 sighted subjects, 10 years of age, was administered conservation of volume tests; 45 percent of these subjects gave correct answers: i.e., affirmed conservation of volume after the specified deformations. Only 5.9 percent of the 11-year-old blind group succeeded. Differences between the two groups are significant at the .01 level. Twenty-five percent (25%) of the groups of blind subjects, ages 12 and 13, were successful; their performance, however, did not differ significantly from the 10-year-old sighted group.

As expected, the time-lag between the achievement of conservation of volume by blind and by sighted subjects is just as great as it was for the conservation of substance and of weight. However, it is again noted that many blind youngsters are unaware of the physical phenomenon evidenced by the rise of the level of a liquid when an object is immersed in it.

Comparison of the Congenitally Blind and Adventitiously Blind

The above tests were administered to 15 adventitiously blind subjects aged seven-to-11 years, and through use of the Sign Test their performance was compared with that of a matched group of 15 congenitally blind youngsters which was randomly drawn from the total congenitally blind sample.

In conservation of substance, the AB were superior to the CB at the .03 level. (Sign Test)

In conservation of weight, the AB were superior to the CB at the .05 level. (Sign Test)

Discussion and Conclusion

In the congenitally blind subjects the same progression was noted in the development of the notion of conservation of substance, weight, and volume (with certain reservations) as was observed by Piaget in normal subjects. Also, the reasons advanced by blind subjects were identical to those expressed by sighted subjects. These findings serve to challenge the position taken by some theoreticians who maintain that the "world of the blind" is heterogeneous and fundamentally different from that of the sighted.

We shall now examine the two initial questions which arose concerning these tests: (1) does the homogeneity of perceptual (i.e., tactual) apprehension of substance and weight among the blind eradicate or reduce the time-lag observed among the sighted between their aquisition of the conservation of substance and their later aquisition of conservation of weight? And (2) since the blind are not influenced by visual cues do they achieve conservation of physical quantities sooner than the sighted?

In reference to (1) above, the data obtained provide an unequivocal and also somewhat unexpected answer. Not only do the blind exhibit a difference in ages between the acquisition of the notions of conservation of substance and weight, but the difference is more accentuated than that observed among the sighted: at ages seven-to-eight, respectively, the normal child achieves conservation of substance and of weight, while achievement for the blind occurs at ages 10 and 12-to-13.

The following facts serve to explain the time-lag evidenced by the blind in the achievement of these two notions for conservation:

First, in tactual exploration, length, width, and height, which determine the amount of substance, are more readily perceptible than weight. This is particularly true in the present experiments where small objects are handled (the diameter of the clay ball is approximately 1¾″) and can be explored by one hand or by both hands together. Therefore, for the blind, apprehension of substance contains a degree of simultaneity, although it is not as marked as for the sighted.

Acquisition of the notion of conservation of weight is more complex because the sensory impressions which correspond to the different weighing operations are subject to more confusing illusions and deformations than those in apprehension of the conservation of substance. Indeed, when held in the hands, two objects identical in weight, but differing in shape *appear* to be of different weights: e.g., a sheet of metal seems lighter than a ball, two small metal balls placed at the extremities of the palm of the hand seem lighter than one big ball placed in the center. Changes in shape not only modify the perceptual appearance of the object, but also modify the subjective impression of weight attached to it. According to Piaget, the greater discrepancies in the evaluation of weights would explain why it takes longer for the "decentration" to occur in the case of weight than in the case of substance.

This reason for delayed achievement also holds for the blind. Even if the quantity of substance is apprehended tactually, and the sausage seems to contain more (or less) clay than the ball, the sensory impressions of the blind do not result in the kind of false "confirmation" that occurs in the subjective sensation of weight provided by two objects of different shape. Both blind and sighted children have negate the false relationship between shape and quantity of substance to arrive at the notion of conservation of substance; but they have to overcome *two* fallacious relationships in the case of weight: the relationship shape/quantity-of-weight, and the false subjective sensation of weighing by the hand. This could explain why, even in the case of blindness, the acquisition of the notions of conversation of substance and weight are not simultaneous.

Actually, the real problem is to understand why it takes only a few months for the sighted child to progress from the notion of conservation to the other, while it takes over two years for the blind child to achieve equivalent understanding.

Before considering possible interpretation, it must first be determined whether or not there is experimental bias due to either an error in sampling or misunderstanding of the instructions.

Bias in sampling, in blind and sighted subjects, can be checked by observing performances of the two groups on tests administered simultaneously during the same session: verbal classification and verbal seriation tests, both described in Chapter VI, pages 00 and 00. The sighted subjects exhibited only slight superiority over the blind ones on the classification test, while the two groups had identical performances on the seriation test. One may interpret these data as indicating that the sighted subjects did not have a particularly high level of intelligence.

The blind subjects did not appear to misunderstand the instructions; therefore, this source of bias does not seem valid. The attitude and verbal reactions of the subjects during the tests left no doubt about their familiarity with the notion of weight. As later noted in Chapter VI, a second group of blind subjects (not the group used in the test of conservation) showed no particular difficulties in a seriation of weight test.

Consequently, the problem remains: Why is the progression from the notion of conservation of substance to the one of weight so much slower among blind subjects than among sighted ones?

One hypothesis considers the influence of school training. It is remembered that when blind and sighted subjects are equated on chronological age or even on mental age the blind subjects show an average academic lag of two years. The lag can be attributed to such factors as late entrance into school, slow academic progression because of the Braille graphic system, etc. A group of sighted children, age eight, is composed of second or third graders, while a group of blind children is composed of kindergarten or first grade students. At that age, the sighted children have learned to solve various measurement problems, particularly weight, while the blind children are just beginning to learn to read and write and to perform very basic operations. It is possible that the sighted have already experienced academic training which permits the extension of logical structure to different content.

This reason can be reversed, however. If the rate of academic progression in classes for blind children is slower than in classes for sighted ones, it is due not only to the technical factors related to the complexity of Braille writing or reading, but also to the incapacity of these children to assimilate notions beyond their operatory and logical level.

After observing blind children, another hypothetical explanation, which supplements the preceding one, seems more acceptable.

If initially, and because of the subjective impressions it evokes, conservation of weight is more difficult than conservation of substance for both blind and sighted children, *blind subjects do not have the ability of sighted ones to check and correct these impressions by objective measurement.* Consider the numberless opportunities a sighted youth has to observe the weight of "compact" or "scattered" objects, and the number of times he has been able, by age eight, to watch the index of a grocery scale and observe that the number of pears required to make up two pounds does not vary as a function of the spatial distribution of these pears, that two small slices of meat of four ounces each are equivalent to one thicker slice of eight ounces, etc. The blind child misses these multiple visual observations, and often does not know until he is 10 or 11 years old how a scale functions, although he may possess a theoretical knowledge of it.

Smedslund (1959;1963) studied the role of empirical controls in the acquisition of the notion of conservation of weight by sighted subjects. His results show that, in general, these controls have little influence on young children; they only aid those who are ready to acquire the notion. Although these controls do not seem to be a sufficient condition in the acquisition of the notion of conservation of weight, they may be considered a necessary condition, and a condition unavailable to blind subjects. This is only one hypothesis which can be tested by comparing blind and sighted children's accuracy in estimating weight and, more importantly, by comparing the development of the errors in both groups.

Whatever the explanation, the maturation necessary for progression from the notion of conservation of substance to the notion of conservation of weight does not occur as rapidly in blind children as in sighted ones. Data to be presented later will show that similar delays in maturation are not observed in other experimental situations. A temporal gradation of acquisitions, similar to the one occurring among sighted children, is not observed among blind subjects; instead, between nine and 11 years of age the blind form a large number of notions almost simultaneously. Extensive coverage is accorded this point in the general conclusions.

Meanwhile, it should be remembered, although explanation is difficult, that the notion of conservation of weight (which, a priori, did not seem to present any particular problems in blindness), surprisingly is acquired much later by blind subjects.

Although it is relatively easy to explain the difficulties encountered by blind children in the preceding study of spatial operations, it is more difficult to explain the nature of those presently discussed. Deprivation of sight does constitute a serious handicap to self-displacements by the subject as well as to his perception of moving objects; but it does not seem to hinder actions based on the notions of conservation of physical quantities. As part of the school's manual-dexterity training program all the blind subjects had various opportunities to handle clay. They were familiar with the many types of lengthening, flattening, sectioning, gathering together of sectioned parts, etc., required in reproducing common objects, animals, or persons. It was the same for all actions of this kind relating to different materials.

Obviously, this does not imply that performance of blind children is equivalent to that of sighted ones in these areas. Because it curtails visual perception and because the child reacts to this curtailment, blindness diminishes the activity of very young children, particularly their constructive activities. Lack of activity or lack of interaction with the surrounding environment can partially, but not totally, explain the deficiencies noted in the blind subjects used in the present study.

It will be shown in the chapters which follow that this decline in activity (which is characteristic not only of blindness but of any physical deficiency) has accompanying difficulties which vary in degree depending on the tasks studied. All these tasks involve operative processes; i.e., they are, according to Piaget's definition, coordinated and reversible actions either real or internalized.

For example, operations involved in the seriation of weights are influenced just as much by the activity of the subject as are the operations involved in conservation; however, in both these instances the inferiority of the blind subjects is less tangible than in the type of operations discussed above.

To understand the origin of the general delay which appeared in the acquisition of physical invariants by the blind subjects, it is necessary to realize that, in Piaget's terminology, physical as well as spatial operations are "infralogical." Bear in mind that this term does not mean "less logical" than logico-mathematical operations.

A certain form of spatial composition is involved in the conservation of quantities. The child is faced with transformations which actually are only *displacements of parts,* and these displacements must be related to the physical quantity of substance or of weight composing the total object. The review of the literature and the experimental results in preceding chapters underline the serious difficulties that the blind experience in the mental construction of the notion of space. The important deficit observed among blind subjects in tests of conservation may, perhaps, be related to their insufficiences in the spatial plane. Either the spatial handicap is the direct cause of their difficulty in the constitution of physical invariants, or both have a common origin which could well be the limitation of their tactual perception. When the findings of Oleron and Herron (1961), which relate to deaf subjects, are compared with ours it is noted that they, too, found a decided delay in the acquisition of conservation of quantity and weight. The average delay of six years noted in the deaf-mute surpassed that observed among blind children. Even the technical and experimental difficulties experienced by the deaf subjects cannot account for such a massive delay. For them, conservation "is a *concept* that the subject must learn, rather than extricate from experimental situations" (Oleron and Herron, 1961, p. 217). When there is a conflict between concrete perceptions and abstract relationships, deaf subjects are systematically handicapped because they continue to be governed by the perceptual aspect, or "perceptual level" of things. These difficulties accentuate the "intellectual character of conservation"; "if conservation was derived from immediate experience or was learned directly from it alone, this time-lag would not exist. Indeed, when the required tasks can be solved by the use of perceptual and perceptual-motor schemes, deaf subjects are not seriously handicapped"; "but when the perceptual motor framework no longer suffices and subjects require superior processes whose development is facilitated by language, the deaf show an inferiority" (Oleron, 1957, p. 218).

The situation of blind subjects is diametrically opposed: they possess the essentially symbolic instrument which language represents; their insufficiency occurs at the concrete and perceptual motor level. Language does not permit them to overcome totally the difficulties which arise from their restricted perceptual contact with things, but their symbol system does account for their superiority over deaf subjects. Possession by the blind child of a system of verbal signs which allow him to overcome the immediate present is more "useful" than the possession by the deaf child of a perceptive system which is capable of providing a variety of simultaneous data. The blind child's use of this verbal system is discussed later.

If, as posited by Smedslund, conservation depends "on one's ability to resist the influence of the figurative field" (Oleron, 1957), then the blind subject who uses only tactual cues is more resistant to this influence than the sighted one. On the contrary, blind children remain at the level of non-conservation longer because of this limitation in their perceptual experience and because of the labile nature of their tactile-kinesthetic cues.

Chapter Six

LOGICAL OPERATIONS:
Classification and Seriation

Contrary to spatial and physical infralogical operations, which center on the object itself, logical operations center on relations *between* given objects and are independent of the spatio-temporal disposition of these objects.

Present consideration is devoted to two major categories of logical operations: (1) operations which require figurative support (i.e., those which involve manipulation of concrete objects); and (2) operations with reduced or no figurative support (i.e., those which bear essentially on verbal content).

The hypotheses which involve logical experiments are:

1. Congenitally blind subjects will show retardation in all logical operations which require concrete manipulaton of objects; however, this time-lag will not be as pronounced as the delay in spatial and physical infralogical operations;

1. Performance of congenitally blind subjects will approximate that of the sighted in verbal logical operations.

Figurative

Consideration is accorded classifications and seriations which involve concrete manipulable material.

Classification

Modes of classification are at the core of "conceptual thought" and of all cognitive activity. Mental illness, as well as natural aging, can affect the capacity to group objects according to common qualities. This capacity is quite fragile, and is one that the deaf have particular difficulty in acquiring because of the role which language plays in the formation of categories. But what is the role of perceptual factors in such an activity?

According to Piaget, the abstraction of common qualities, a process basic to classification, does not derive directly from the perceptual apprehension of physical qualities. It generates from actions on these objects, actions which are progressively coordinated and grouped in reversible systems. When a young child is given a complex group of objects to classify, he starts making "figurative collections" based on irrelevant elements rather than engaging in true classification. These figurative collections originate from a lack of coordination between the comprehension of the class (i.e., the definition of the quality or qualities common to the members of the class) and the extension of the class (the number of things that can be grouped under that class). The figurative collections disappear progressively and are replaced, first by intuitive classifications, then by operatory classifications based on one or several criteria.

Coordination between comprehension and extension cannot be accomplished by purely perceptual means and, according to Piaget, is realized only through logical operations. The perception of common qualities is not sufficient for the constitution of classes; in fact, it may even be a handicap if these perceptions conflict with the conceptual category which has to be formed. Oleron states that the deficiency observed among deaf subjects in tasks of multiple classifications is caused by this type of conflict: because of their total or partial deprivation of language, the deaf cannot disengage themselves from what they perceive, particularly if differences between objects are more numerous and more visible than resemblances. For this reason the deaf child is slow in his progression from what Oleron terms the "perceptual" to the "conceptual," or categorical, level.

A similar reason is advanced by Piaget as he interprets the results of an experiment comparing young children's performances on a task which required classification through visual versus tactile-kinesthetic perception (Piaget, 1959). When children worked from behind a screen, tactile-kinesthetic exploration did not hamper their ability to perform classifications involving one or several criteria. On the contrary, Piaget noted a slight superiority among subjects who used only tactile perception when compared to subjects who worked normally through visual-tactile-kinesthetic channels. Because of the fragmentary and successive nature of tactual decision, perception derived only from exploratory and relational activity, and resulted in superior performances.

Discovery of Law of Classification
Based on Perceptual Contrast

This task, adapted from Piaget and Inhelder (1959), is an oddity problem. In the experiment a group of objects is presented; all are identical except for one, which is markedly different. The object which is different is marked on the back; the others are not. All objects are presented to the child face up, and he is required to decide which object contains the mark on the back; as he successfully identified it on successive attempts he induces a law of classification; he classifies one object as unique.

According to Piaget and Inhelder, such a discovery is possible as early as six to seven years of age, because understanding is based in part on the perceptual organization of the material or on sensory-motor learning. By contrast, the operatory notion of class does not occur until later (8–9 years). Using this type of experiment Inhelder has found that in some cases perceptual organization factors aid reasoning, while in others (conservation, for example) they are the main obstacle to operativity (Inhelder, 1956, pp. 138–139).

In adapting this experiment for use with young blind children it was hypothesized that these children would not perform as well as sighted children of the same age because the tactile-kinesthetic apprehension of the material is much less structured than the visual apprehension.

Description of material

Material consists of numbers of pieces of wood which differ in shape, dimension, and texture. In Series I, perceptual contrast is based on shape; in Series II, on texture; in Series III, on size; and in Series IV, on direction.

Series I: Contrast in shape: Three pieces of wood identical in shape, size, and texture, and one piece which is quite different in shape are presented to the child; the differing piece is marked on the back with a distinctive sign (which can be perceived tactually). During each of a succession of presentations, the child must guess which piece is marked on the back.

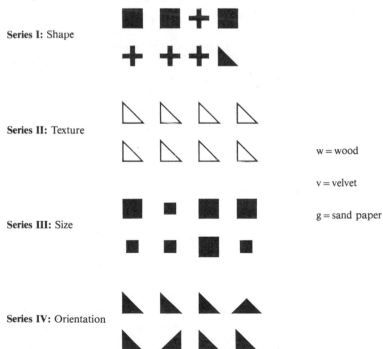

Fig. 12 Examples of shape, texture, size, and orientation combinations.

Series II: Contrast in texture: Shape and size are constant, but the object with the mark on the back is of a different texture. (Objects are of painted wood, or are covered with velvet or sandpaper.)

Series III: Contrast in size: Shape and texture are constant, but the object with the mark on the back differs in size.

Series IV: Contrast in orientation: Shape, texture, and size are constant, but the object with the mark on the back is placed so that its orientation differs from that of the other three.

Figure 12 gives two examples of combinations for each series.

Technique and instructions

After the child becomes familiar with the material he is introduced to a play situation and told "in order to win you must guess which piece of wood has a mark on the back." He is also told that "there is a way to find out just which piece of wood has the mark on the back and is the winning one." He is promised a piece of candy at the end of the game if he discovers how to determine the correct one. (Actually, each subject is given a piece of candy regardless of whether or not he discovers the method.) If the subject chooses the wrong piece he is asked to check and see if it has a mark on the back (he thereby discovers his error); after that piece is returned to the group he is told to choose from the other three the one he thinks is marked; the procedure is repeated until he identifies the correct one. Each time the right piece is chosen on the first guess the subject receives a reward.

The four series are always presented in the order described above. The limited number of blind subjects did not permit comparison of performance on one series with performance on another. Instead, total scores were used.

Criterion for "passing" performance for a series is five consecutive right answers. If criterion is not reached during the presentation of the twelve items comprising that series the subject proceeds to the next series.

At the end of the test, and regardless of the results, the child is asked to justify his choices. (How did you guess? What was the way never to be wrong?)

Subjects using tactual perception were required to conduct a thorough exploration on each round of presentation. The subject's answer was not accepted until all four objects had had extensive tactual exploration.

To assure that the subject's tactual exploration would not alter or disarrange the configuration, the four pieces of wood were attached to a larger block of wood just prior to presentation.

Sample

The task was administered to congenitally blind children (CB), to sighted children working in visual perception (SV), and to sighted children working in tactual perception from behind a screen (ST).

The number of subjects tested by category and by age is set forth in Table 4.

Table 4
Number of SV, ST, and CB subjects
Ages five through ten

CA	5	6	7	8	9	10
SV...	22	22	24	25		
ST...			21	20	18	
CB...			11	20	14	10

Results

1. *Median number of successfully completed series*: The median number of successes (criterion reached regardless the verbal justification given later by the child) is shown in Table 5:

Table 5
Median number of successfully completed series

CA	5	6	7	8	9	10
SV...	.35	3.57	4.00	4.00		
ST...			.75	3.16	3.33	
CB...			.11	.27	2.00	3.00

a. *Comparison of SV and CB*: Review of Table 5 indicates performance of CB subjects is four years below that of SV subjects. Also, it is noted that differences at 10 years in the performance of CB subjects is not significantly different from that SV subjects at six years. But differences are significant at the .05 level between six-year SV and nine-year CB subjects (Median test).

b. *Comparison of ST and CB*: The comparison is of interest because even when the sighted subjects work on tasks requiring tactual perception (i.e. are placed temporarily in a situation identical to that of the blind subjects) they still benefit from all their past experiences which derive from visual representation. Their performance is superior to that of congenitally blind subjects. This superiority is not as great as it is when sighted subjects work on tasks of visual perception (SV). Indeed, when the two groups are of equivalent age, differences between ST and CB are significant, but differences are non-significant when eight-year-old CB's are compared with seven-year-old ST's or nine-year-old CB's with eight-year-old ST's.

c. *Comparison of ST and SV*: The performance of ST is systematically and significantly inferior to that of SV. Performance of the ST group is located midway between that of the SV and CB groups.

d. *Comparison of congenitally and adventitiously blind subjects*: The 11 adventitiously blind subjects, ages seven to 10 years (average age = nine years, five months), were matched (as closely as possible) with congenitally blind subjects included in the initial sampling. The superiority of the AB is significant at .005 level (Wilcoxon test).

2. *Discovery of the general law.* The subject was credited with having discovered the law if his answer indicated he addressed attention to the uniqueness of the object: e.g., "It's the one which is by itself," "It's the one which is not like the others," It's the one which is not the same," etc. If his answer indicated consideration only of particular aspects then it was regarded as a partial discovery: e.g., "The one which doesn't have the same shape," "The one which doesn't have the same dimension," etc. The number of subjects who discovered the general law, the number who discovered the partial law, and finally the number of those who failed totally was determined (Fig. 13). When comparison of the three groups is based on subjects of equal age, all differences are significant. Again, the performance of ST is mid-way between that of SV and of CB. Performance of CB is an average of three years below that of the SV (but differences between six-year-old SV's and nine-year-old CB's are not significant).

Mean Percentage

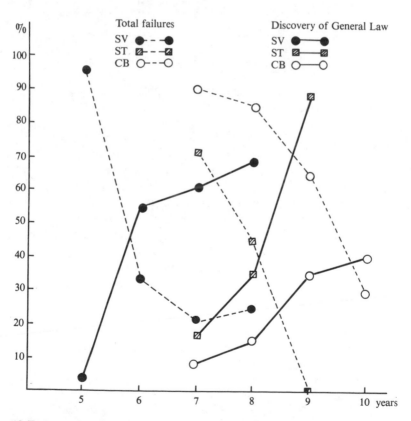

Fig. 13 Percentage of total success and failures on the experiment involving the discovery of a law based on perceptive contrast.

Comparison of the CB and AB: When comparison was made of the matched groups of AB and CB on their ability to formulate a general law, differences which favored the AB were significant at the .01 level.

3. *Correlation between the number of series successfully completed and the discovery of the general law.* The degree of relationship between the number of successfully completed series and answers which indicated discovery of the law is of interest. The contingency coefficient is .40 for the SV group, .50 for the ST group, and .58 for the CB group; all are significant at the .001 level, but differences between groups are not significant.

4. *Comparison of the retrolental fibroplasia subjects with blind subjects of different etiology.* The question here is "Does the high proportion of retrolental fibroplasia subjects in the congenitally blind group affect the results?" Again, as in the spatial operations experiment, it is important to consider etiology in the analysis of results.

The 17 fibroplasia subjects (from seven to ten years of age) in the CB group were matched with CB subjects whose blindness was attributed to other causes.

The median for the number of series successfully completed is .92 for the retrolental fibroplasia group, and .94 for the non-retrolental fibroplasia group. Also, differences in the ability of the two groups to discover the general law are non-significant. In other words, no difference is observed when the performance of the group of prematures is compared to that of the group which has different etiologies. Therefore, blindness rather than prematurity appears to be the influencing factor.

Summary and Conclusions

The results obtained from this particular experiment confirm the general hypothesis: (1) performance of congenitally blind subjects when compared with SV (visual perception) subjects reflects a delay of three to four years; (2) performance of ST (sighted-tactual perception) subjects is midway between the SV and the CB. Some of their difficulties can be attributed to momentary use of tactile-kinesthetic rather than visual channels. However, the ST continue to benefit from earlier visual representations, and during the experiment their behavior indicates that they systematically proceed to "translate" their tactual impressions into visual imagery representations. Thus, their present experimentally-imposed handicap is less penalizing than the permanent handicap of the congenitally blind subjects; (3) finally, congenitally blind subjects are significantly inferior to adventitiously blind ones.

To evaluate these results, it is necessary to analyse the psychological processes required by the task. To find the right answers, there are three necessary conditions: (1) First, the child must *perceive a difference* between the unique object (the only one of its kind) and the identical objects forming the configuration. Care was taken to insure that perceptual contrasts were marked rather than marginal; doubtless all subjects observed the fact that one of the pieces of wood was different from the other three; (2) The second condition concerns the regular and systematic character of this difference. The child must decide that the general structure of the configuration is regular: i.e., that there is *always* a different object among three identical ones; and (3) Finally, the fact that one object is always different from the others must also be related to the distinctive mark which makes one object unique: i.e., "the winner." There is need to determine why identification occurs at an earlier age if the material is visual, and why blind subjects and sighted ones working from behind a screen encounter so much difficulty in tasks which required tactile-kinesthetic perceptions.

Consideration is addressed to the structuration of material, a factor which is viewed by Inhelder (1955) as a facilitator. In visual perception the structure of the collection of objects remains constant during its whole presentation, and also during the child's period of reflection and during the time the examiner pronounces his answer as correct—"win"—or incorrect—"lost." By contrast, the perceptual structure of the material is less pronounced in tactual perception and manifests itself only during the initial exploration; although the initial exploration is complete and systematic it may fade or even disappear after the choice is made: if the child moves his fingers even slightly the pieces of wood leave his field of apprehension, and consequently their "perceptual existence" is lost.

Contrary to what might be expected, deprivation of sight does not generate an increase in tactual-motor activity. On the contrary, there is a general tendency toward passivity among these subjects. Their exploration is partial, unorganized, and, in the young, incoherent. Such unsystematic exploration only aggravates the difficulties inherent in tactual apprehension by accentuating its fragmentation and liability.

Be that as it may, the results of the experiment suggest that "what catches the eye does not as easily catch the hands." The poorer performance of sighted subjects working from behind a screen (but who have the use, theoretically, of the same intellectual abilities as the ones working in visual perception) shows the extent to which the processes on which they based their performances implies a reasoning which remains dependent on the perceptual structuration of the situation. Data from research on animals, which involved learning experiences of this type substantiate and extend the findings (Young and Harlow, 1943).

Performance of blind subjects, which is inferior to that of ST subjects, supplies evidence of the facilitating role of perceptual factors in certain types of reasoning. These findings will be discussed again later when comparison is made of blind and sighted subjects' perfomances on a test which parallels this one in principle and structure, but which employs a law of classification based on semantic contrast, not on perceptual contrast (see Chapter 6). Because quite different results were obtained for the two groups in these two experiments there will be further discussion of the psychological significance and value of our present observations.

Classification of Geometric Forms and Shifting Criterion

In the preceding experiment the child has to discover the principle involved in the classification of objects presented to him. Another frequently used procedure, which involves the inverse method, consists of presenting the subject with a collection of heterogeneous objects and asking him to "invent" an adequate mode of classification. This latter approach is used in assessments designed by Goldstein and Sheerer, and Weigl.

Principle

The following experiment is adapted from Piaget and Inhelder's work (1958). In it the child is presented with a certain number of pieces of wood and told to group them in two categories. Three types of grouping are possible: (1) shape (square or round), (2) size (large or small), and (3) thickness (thick or thin). After the child groups or classifies the objects in one criterion he is asked to change criterion: i.e., to discover other categories.

The ability to reorganize previously-organized structures is viewed as important by Goldstein. According to him, this ability is characteristic of adult reasoning as opposed to reasoning of the child or the mentally ill. Because it deprives the young child of all visual perceptions, does blindness modify his capacities for classification?

Description of material (Fig. 14)

Eight pieces of wood, composed of:

1. *Two cubes*: one measuring $\frac{5}{8}$″ on each side, the other $1\frac{5}{8}$″;
2. *Two flat squares* measuring $\frac{5}{8}$″ in thickness, one $2\frac{5}{8}$″ on each side, the other $1\frac{5}{8}$″;
3. *Two spheres*: one measuring $2\frac{5}{8}$″ in diameter, the other $1\frac{5}{8}$″;
4. *Two flat discs* measuring $\frac{5}{8}$″ in thickness, one $2\frac{5}{8}$″ in diameter, the other $1\frac{5}{8}$″.

Fig. 14

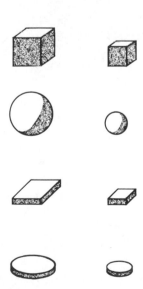

Technique

After the child has thoroughly explored the material he is told to sort these eight pieces of wood into the two boxes in such a way that each box will contain things "which go together, which look a little bit a like, which could be of the same family." Then he is asked why he sorted them as he did: i.e., he explains the criterion he used in his classification ("how do these pieces of wood look alike? why do they go together?").

Then he is asked to make a second grouping using a different criterion ("another way"), then a third one. Each time he states the reason for sorting them as he did. If, during the test, a blind subject leaves one of the pieces on the table, the examiner calls his attention to it.

Sample

Table 6 indicates the number of SV, ST, and CB subjects participating in the experiment.

Table 6.
Number of Subjects Administered the Test of Geometric Classification

CA	6	7	8	9	10	11
SV...	17	23	21	22	18	
ST...		20	20	17		
CB...			17	17	16	10

Results

1. *Preliminary note*: A classification response is correct when it meets two requirements: (1) distribution of the pieces of wood in the two boxes must conform to the classification criterion: i.e., *no error is accepted*; (2) the child must be able to *justify* his classification: i.e., to explain the similarity between objects placed in the same box. During the initial interview of subjects the need for the second requirement became apparent. Although certain subjects made classifications that appeared correct, later, as they discussed their actions, they stated that the eight objects had been divided into four categories, not into two: in fact, each box contained two sub-groups separated by an imaginary partition. For example, if a subject used shape as the criterion (squares and circles) he would place separately, but within the same box, cubes and flat squares, and when questioned failed to see any similarity between them. For this reason the subjects' verbalized reason for or explanation of the classification he has just carried out is important.

2. *Percentages of subjects who discover one, two, or three criteria of classification*: The percentage of subjects in each age group who classified successfully on one, two, or all three criteria is set forth in Figure 15. The following analysis is derived from these data:

Note: Figure 15 appears on page 133

First, there is no difference between the SV and ST groups. Piaget's suggestion that tactual-kinesthetic apprehension should promote abstraction because it stimulated activity (Piaget and Inhelder, 1959, p. 246) is not confirmed. Although he is not "submerged" by visual perceptual data, the ST child does not perform better or demonstrate more "flexibility" than the SV subject. In this type of task, however, the lack of *actual* visual data does not represent a handicap; at least, it does not for persons the ages of those used in the present study. With younger subjects, the behavior of SV and ST may differ significantly, although it would be very difficult for young children to meet the experimental demands made of the ST subjects: i.e., to use only tactual perceptual and to work from behind a screen during the entire test period. Inability of younger subjects to perform in this manner caused them to be eliminated from the study. However, SV and ST subjects, ages seven and up, have identical performances.

Second, the situation created by congenital blindness results in a completely different performance. In short, the performance of blind subjects is clearly inferior to that of sighted ones (both SV and ST):

a. When subjects from the two groups are equated on age the differences between blind and sighted subjects are significant (at the .01 level for eight year olds, and at the .001 for nine and ten year olds) (X^2).

b. Even when the blind are one year older—i.e., when nine-year-old blind subjects are compared with eight-year-old sighted ones—the differences are still significant at .01 level (X^2).

c. When the blind are two years more advanced in age—i.e., when ten-year-old blind subjects are compared two eight-year-old sighted ones—the differences are no longer significant (X^2).

In other words, when congenitally blind subjects are compared to the sighted ones the performance of the blind on this test presents an average time-lag of two years.

3. *Use of different criteria.* Are the three criteria—shape, thickness, and size—used in equal proportion: i.e., is one of them, particularly shape, chosen more often? Also, are there differences between the SV, ST, and CB groups in the frequency with which one particular criterion is selected?

For subjects who used only one criterion the percentage of those who classified according to (1) shape, (2) size, and (3) thickness was determined. Figure 16 shows that, among six-year-old SV subjects, 60 percent of those who could use only one criterion classified in terms of shape; the remaining 40 percent was almost evenly divided between the other two criteria, size and thickness. At later ages the percentage classifying on shape increased to between 80 percent and 90 percent for ST as well as SV subjects. 55 percent of the eight- and nine-year-old CB subjects classified according to shape, and 90 percent of the ten-year-old CB subjects did.

Thus, a similar pattern of responses is observed in blind and sighted subjects; the difference lies in the age delay for the blind group.

4. *Comparison of AB and CB.* As in earlier experiments, this test was administered to a group of ten AB subjects, ages seven to ten, and their performance was compared to that of a matched group of ten CB subjects which was randomly

selected from the total sample. The difference between their performances was significant at the .001 level. Again, the AB subjects had the superior performance.

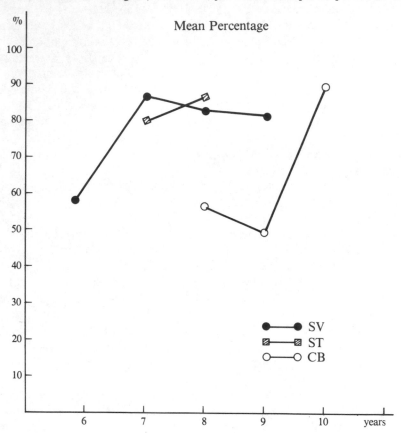

Fig. 16 Percentage of subjects classifying according to shape (among those who used only one criterion of classification).

Conclusions

The delay observed in the congenitally blind when they were compared to sighted subjects, as well as the superiority of the adventitiously over the congenitally blind subjects, confirms our original hypothesis: disturbance at the level of perceptual apprehension caused by total and early deprivation of visual information influences later activities generally considered "abstract"; and in which the perceived data may, at times, actually conflict with reasoning.

For example, Oleron attributes the difficulties encountered by deaf youths in tests of multiple classifications to deprivation or insufficiency of language which leads them to attach too much importance to visually perceived appearance and emphasizes the material or spatial organization of objects. For this reason, the mental activity of deaf-mute subjects "tends to remain at a level where perceived elements are not sufficiently subordinated to concepts; thus, this level is termed 'perceptual' '' (Oleron, 1952, p. 131).

Language, according to Oleron, allows the child to go beyond the immediate and material existence of things; it promotes passage to the "conceptual" level and to the generality of class. Oleron's experiments are not strictly comparable to those presently used: average age of his deaf subjects was 15 years, and his experimental material was much more complex than that used in this study. Most of the difficulties encountered by Oleron's subjects involved shifting: i.e., changing criteria. Deaf subjects could sort on one criterion equally as well as hearing subjects of comparable age, but when the task required abandonment of that criterion and initiation of a new form of sorting they did not perform as well as hearing subjects. By contrast, congenitally blind children succeed in their first classification attempt much later than sighted subjects.

Interpretation of this difference in behavior is difficult because of the age difference between our blind subjects and the deaf children in Oleron's experimental sample. It would be necessary to know if young deaf children encounter difficulty in classifying in terms of only one category when the objects to be classified differ in several aspects (shape, color, dimension, etc.). Also, one may wonder if the difficulties in classification initially experienced by blind children do not disappear as they grow older, particularly when the various possible classifications are based on criteria as simple and familiar as shape or size.

Whatever it may be, the time-lag observed among congenitally blind subjects in our test of classification evokes certain problems, particularly when consideration is given the respective roles of language and perception in the development of classificatory activity.

Blindness does not interfere with the development of language, at least not with its mechanism of acquisition and its instrumental role of "doubling" reality. But early deprivation of sight considerably reduces the quantity and the nature of sensory information which reaches the blind subject, and it also reduces his perceptual knowledge of exterior objects. In other words, he is placed in a situation diametrically opposed to that of the deaf subject who, because of his visual experiences, has a rich and differentiated perceptual knowledge, but who has difficulty in establishing a verbal system. The blind child, on the contrary, handles language with great ease, but the visual perception of objects is denied him.

Because, as both Piaget and Oleron have noted, the blind are relieved of "fidelity to the visually perceived", one might assume that their performance would be equal (or perhaps superior) to that of the sighted since they are less influenced by the visible aspects of things but can employ the verbal conceptual instrument. Nonetheless, the reverse is true: perceptual impressions are still the main system of reference for the blind child. The fact that these impressions are partial, unstructured, or, at times, truly incoherent, does not modify their importance for the youngest children, and does not encourage the appearance of higher level behaviors. Despite the integrity of his linguistic system, the blind subject remains attached to his limited perceived impressions, as do the deaf subjects and the younger sighted ones.

Study of deficiencies in the blind and deaf provide clarification of the role of language in logical behavior at the concrete level. If the difficulties observed among deaf subjects can be explained by their verbal deficiency alone, then for the normal child (who can see and hear), language in tasks involving concrete material plays the role of "accelerator" of conceptual development *only* when it is based on a sufficiently rich and differentiated ground at the level of perceptual knowledge. Deficiencies of both deaf and blind subjects show that progress is swift only when there is concomitant integrity of the perceptual system and integrity of the verbal one.

Comparison of the performances of the blind and deaf on a multiple classifications class would determine if the impairment of perceptual knowledge in the blind and the lack of language in the deaf have equivalent effects, or if one condition is more handicapping than the other. To our knowledge, McAndrew (1948), who studied rigidity within the framework of Lewin's theory, is the only person who has compared performance of groups of deaf, blind, and normal children, ages 10 to 14, on a series of tests which included multiple classification (i.e., 25 objects were classified according to shape—squares, circles, triangles, etc.—and substance—cardboard, cork, leather, glass, etc.) Performance of deaf subjects was inferior to that of normals, while blind subjects were superior to the deaf and only slightly inferior to the normal (but scoring was based on the number of trials, not on the change of criterion). McAndrew viewed these results as confirming her hypothesis that rigidity (which was seen as dependent on the individual's degree of social isolation) would be more pronounced among deaf subjects than among blind ones, and in turn, more pronounced among blind subjects than among normal ones.

But, when reviewing McAndrew's results, one must remember that she uses the legal definition of blindness: i.e., an individual is blind if his vision is equal to or less than 20/200. The definition may be appropriate if one is concerned with the affective or social aspects of the sensory deficiency, but it is not appropriate in the study of cognitive processes, particularly when these processes are based, in varying degrees, on perceptual information. It is possible that McAndrew's selection of blind and sighted subjects allowed too much variation in the blind sample.

The term "rigidity" is often employed to account for difficulties which certain groups have in shifting or changing modes of classification. However, some experimental controls must be established before use of the concept is appropriate. Indeed, two aspects in the successful achievement of multiple classifications tests must be distinguished. The first, a cognitive one, is concerned with the different possible criteria of classification. In general, degree of difficulty varies in terms of the degree of visibility of the common characteristic on which the classification is based. For example, at a certain age, classification by color is more frequent (and consequently "easier") than that by shape or dimension (Vincent, 1957). Similarly, Heidbredder has presented evidence of a hierarchical order in the formation of concepts of concrete objects, geometrical shapes, and numbers (1948).

The second aspect, based on personality or individual differences, is concerned with the typically "rigid" or "flexible" attitude of the subject attempting the classification: i.e., his capacity for "restructuring" the field.

To speak of rigidity in experiments of this kind requires that the various possible criteria be of equal difficulty: i.e., at a given age or for a given population, the several criteria have equal chances to appear in a spontaneous classification. Real rigidity then would be the incapacity of a subject to break up the perceptual structure of his first mode of classification and adopt another one that would be based on the same level of "abstraction" as the first one. Only then would rigidity refer to an individual personality trait not directly determined by intellectual and cognitive capacities. Because of these factors a consideration of rigidity is not a part of our study.

Rather, it is emphasized that classification according to one or several criteria presents more difficulty for the blind than for the sighted child. There also is note that the deficiency exhibited by the blind subjects on this test is not as great as the deficiency they exhibited when the classification was based on perceptual contrast. When perceptual contrast was involved a four-year delay was observed, whereas the average delay was two years in experiments which required a higher level of abstraction, a level not closely related to a perceptual configuration.

Seriation

The seriation task requires the ordering of a series of increasingly larger or increasingly smaller items: i.e., A>B, B>C, C>D, etc. Contrary to classification, seriation is "oriented": i.e., the position of any two elements is not interchangeable within the series. It is termed the "asymmetry," or "orientation," of ordinal relationship: if x is larger than y, then y cannot be larger than x.

But the most fundamental property of ordinal relationship is its transitivity: if $x<y$ and if $y<z$, then $x<z$.

Children's ability to engage in seriation has been studied for some time. Many educational games for pre-school children are composed of series of objects with ordinal relationship (cubes, balls, cups, nested eggs, etc.); but learning to order such a series of objects does not involve all the aspects of operatory seriation. In instances where a new element is placed correctly within a series which is already constructed it is necessary to determine the position where the new object will be inferior to all the preceding ones and superior to all the following ones.

On the psychological level, seriation and classification differ on one essential point: there is no perception of a class, per se, but there is perception of a series. Does the perception of serial adjustments facilitate the operative development of seriations? Piaget and Inhelder (1959) think not, since classification and seriation appear at approximately the same age (7–8 years), and since both are based on sensory-motor activities, in general, and not on the isolated perception of series in particular.

There was interest in comparing performance of our blind and sighted experimental groups on tests of seriations to determine if the perceptive limitations imposed by blindness generate difficulties in this kind of task, or if they have no specific effect. To do this, tasks were included which required the seriation of three types of material:

1. Seriation of cubes that vary on all three dimensions—length, width, and height;

2. Seriation of little wooden sticks—the width of the sticks is constant, only their length varies;

3. Seriation of weights—the objects are identical visually, only their weight varies.

If, as implied in our hypothesis, perceptual cues facilitate the task of ordering concrete objects, then we can forecast:

a. that the seriation of cubes will be the task most easily accomplished, seriation of sticks the next, and seriation of weights the most difficult (generally, this was what was observed);

b. blind subjects will be handicapped if the series is perceived in a global and simultaneous fashion: i.e., their performance in the seriation of cubes or sticks will be poorer than in the seriation of weights because their perception of weight is similar to that of sighted subjects.

Description of Material

Cubes

A series of seven cubes, varying in size from $\frac{7}{8}''$ to $2''$ (with a size progression of $\frac{3}{16}''$, and one $1\frac{1}{4}''$ cube which is to be inserted into the series of seven.

Small Wooden Sticks

Seven small sticks, varying in length from $2\frac{3}{4}''$ to $7\frac{1}{4}''$ for the blind subjects (size progession of $\frac{3}{4}''$); seven small sticks, varying in length from $2\frac{3}{4}''$ to $5''$ for the sighted subjects (size progession of $\frac{3}{8}''$; one stick $4\frac{1}{2}''$ in length to be inserted in the series.

Weights

Seven identical boxes measuring $1\frac{5}{8}'' \ ^4 \ 1\frac{5}{8}'' \ ^4 \ \frac{5}{8}''$, the weights of which vary from 10 grams to 57 grams with a constant ratio of .75.

Technique

At the opening of the experiment the subject is engaged in the seriation of three cubes ("put the biggest cube first, the second largest one next, and the third largest one next, etc."). If the subject does not understand, the examiner demonstrates how "steps can be built with them," and asks him to try again. If the subject seriates the three cubes he is asked to seriate five, and then seven. Finally the subject is given the cube which is to be inserted in the series, and is told "to find where it fits into the group." For each seriation of three, five, and seven elements, as well as for the placing of the inserted element, three trials are permitted.

Sample

Tables 7 and 8 indicate the age range for each group (SV, ST, and CB) included in the experiment.

Table 7
Number of Subjects
Administered Experiments in Seriation of Cubes and Seriation of Sticks

CA	4	5	6	7	8	9
SV...	14	18	17	22		
ST...				20	20	16
CB...			15	15	18	

Table 8
Number of Subjects
Administered the Test of Seriation of Weights

CA	4	5	6	7	8	9
SV...	18	17	22	23	23	15
ST...			20	20	16	
CB...			15	15	18	14

Results

Cotation: The seriation was considered correct if all elements composing the series were correctly placed in at least two of the three trials.

Seriation of Cubes and Sticks

Figure 17 indicates the percentage of subjects who correctly seriated five cubes and seven cubes, and the percentage who correctly inserted the additional item. Figure 18 provides the same type of information on the seriation of sticks.

1. Note that there is no difference between the age seven ST group (working in tactual perception) and the age seven SV group (working in visual perception); at that age, deprivation of sight does not influence performance. It may be that in subjects aged five and six rather than seven the presence of the screen would increase the difficulty of the classification task because the screen tends to eliminate any correction due to perceptual adjustment.

2. Differences in the performance of CB and SV subjects are more obvious. Success of the six- to seven-year-old CB group is approximately equivalent to that of the four-year-old SV on the seriation of cubes and the seriation of sticks. Indeed, differences between five-year-old SV and six- to seven-year-old CB subjects are significant at levels varying from .05 to .002. When the task required the insertion of an additional cube, performance of the six- to seven-year-old CB subjects did not differ significantly from that of the five-year-old SV children, but the superiority of six-year-old SV's over the six- to seven-year-old CB's was

significant at the .01 level. On the seriation of sticks task, superiority of five year-old SV's over eight-year old CB's is significant at .025 level (X^2).

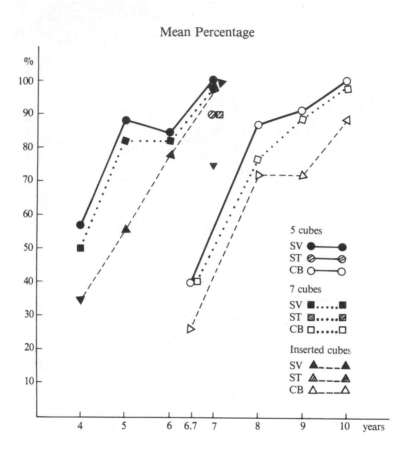

Fig. 17 Percentage of subjects who successfully seriated 5 and 7 cubes and correctly inserted the addtional elements.

Summary. SV subjects show a systematic superiority over CB subjects; differences between groups vary from one to three years.

3. *Comparison of CB and AB.* Age range of the nine adventitiously blind subjects was eight to 10½ years. When their performance was compared with that of a matched group of congenitally blind subjects there were no significant differences. However, lack of significance could be attributed to the near maximum performance of both groups (satisfactory performance was noted for CB subjects).

Mean Percentage

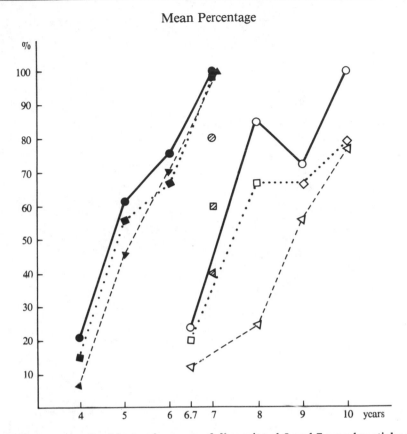

Fig. 18 Percentage of subjects who successfully seriated 5 and 7 wooden sticks and correctly inserted the addtional elements.

5 wooden sticks	7 wooden sticks	Inserted element
SV O——O	SV ■·····■	SV ▲‑‑‑▲
ST ⊘——⊘	ST ▨·····▨	ST ▲‑‑‑▲
CB ●——●	CB □·····□	CB △‑‑‑△

Seriation of Weights:

The percentage of subjects who succeeded in the seration of five and seven elements is shown in Figure 19.

1. As on previous measures the scores for the SV and ST do not differe significantly.

2. When compared with sighted subjects, the CB exhibit a slight delay; the only significant difference between the two groups, however, is in the seriation of five weights at 10 years of age. These results differ from those obtained in the seriation of cubes and of sticks; in these instances the blind subjects were delayed from one to three years. Nonetheless, the findings tend to confirm our general hypotheses: visual perception of material, which is identical in shape and dimension, does not greatly increase the sighted subjects' information, and their performance differs only slightly or not at all from that of the blind subjects.

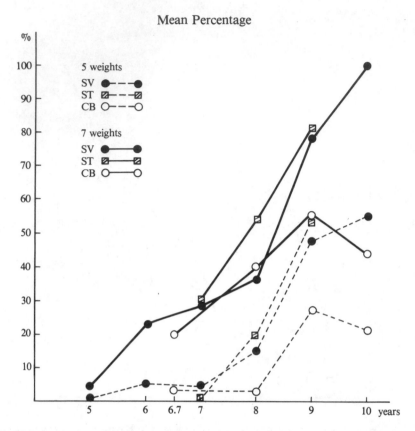

Fig. 19 Percentage of subjects who successfully seriated 5 and 7 weights

3. *Comparison of the congenitally and adventitiously blind*: The seriation of weights was administered to the same nine AB subjects and also to nine CB matched subjects; but in this instance neither group achieved maximum performance although 42 percent of the ten-year-old CB's suceeded in the seriation of five weights and only 25 percent the seriation of seven weights. No significant difference appeared between the CB and AB groups. This lack of significant difference was hypothesized.

Conclusions

The fact that the delay observed among blind subjects in the seriation of cubes and of sticks did not extend to seriation of weights serves to confirm our hypothesis and indicates that the handicap caused by blindness is accentuated in tasks based on visual perception of material. These findings will be referred to later when blind and sighted subjects are compared on a test of oral seriation which does not involve visual or tactual perception.

Comparison of results from seriation of weights with previously-mentioned results on tests of conservation of weight is interesting (Chapter 5). While the performance of blind subjects approximated that of sighted ones in seriation of weights, this was not true on tasks which were based on the notion of physical invariants, particularly when the task was conservation of weight. Although this inconsistency in behaviors was surprising at first, it did indicate that lack of familiarity with the concept of weight was not the only cause of difficulty.

A clear interpretation of these results is possible only through the analysis of the operations involved in each of these two tasks. In the first one, the child is dealing with physical transformations of the object itself: lengthening, flattening, sectioning, bringing sectioned parts back together, etc. Piaget terms these operations "infralogical," not because they are less logical than operations of classification or of seriation (they have exactly the same properties of reversibility and equilibrium), but because they tend to constitute the object itself and promote consideration of spatial relationships (displacement of parts). By comparison, the seriation of a collection of objects involves operations termed "logico-arithmetical" (which also include classification and numerical operations). These logico-arithmetical operations serve to establish relations between given objects, and therefore are independent of the spatial-temporal disposition of these objects. Classification is based on relations of similarity and seriation on relations of difference.

As concerns imagery, physical and spatial infralogical operations are more easily represented than logico-arithmetical operations. Lengthening, sectioning, displacement are directly perceivable by the subject, and therefore are easily imaginable. However, there is no perception of class nor any perception of the relation of ordering (a perception of an ordered series exists, but a perception of the relation itself does not). There also is no perception of number, and the imagery related to numbers has only a faint relationship with the operation itself. According to Piaget, this is why space frequently has been erroneously considered as an "immediate given" already included in perceptions.

Blindness is characterized by a limitation in the perceptual awareness of outside reality, and consequently by an impoverishment of representative imagery. If we accept Piaget's distinction between infralogical and logical operations, blindness would be expected to have different effects on these two types of operations; a greater deficiency would be expected when operations and representative imagery are more highly involved: i.e., in infralogical operations. This is what was found. A difference of more than four years separates blind and sighted subjects in the acquisition of the notion of conservation of weight, but differences between the two groups are negligible in the seriation of weights. The disparity in the ages at which these two types of operation appear in blind subjects and their near simultaneous appearance in sighted subjects suggests that the two operations are not identical in nature.

Verbal

Consideration is accorded to classifications and seriations where figurative support is limited or non-existent.

The findings thus far have indicated that the performance of blind subjects is inferior to that of the sighted. The difference varied from task to task, but with the

The findings thus far have indicated that the performance of blind subjects is inferior to that of the sighted. The difference varied from task to task, but with the exception of seriation of weights, it is always significant. Even in "conceptual" tasks, which involve concrete, manipulable material, the absence of visual representation is a continuing handicap, and at the levels of development included in the present study, the use of tactile-kinesthetic information does not overcome this difficulty.

Interest now turns to the behavior of blind children on tasks for which the concrete and figurative support is limited or absent: i.e., operations with a verbal base. According to our hypothesis, blind subjects should be less handicapped in such operations than in tasks with important figurative support.

Earlier mention (in the discussion of methodological problems in Chapter Three) has been made of the theoretical and practical factors which made it difficult to devise verbal tasks. The tasks used focused on those aspects of classifications and seriations which can be studied in situations which involve minimal handling or concrete representation.

Classification

Discovery of a Law Based on Semantic Contrast

General principle

This experiment corresponds to the previously-discussed one which dealt with the discovery of a law based on perceptual contrast. There it was shown that if the discovery of a law relied heavily on the concrete structuring of the material handled, the blind were gravely handicapped. Intuitive factors which lead to the solution were not as influential in tactile-kinesthetic perception as in visual perception. Now performance of the blind will be compared with that of the sighted in a task whose structuring is identical to the above situation, but whose solution involves verbal contrast rather than perceptual contrast.

In this experiment the subject is supplied a series of words, all of which belong to the same class. An additional word which does not belong is presented; it is termed the "winner." In each case, the child has to discover that the winning word is the word that does not belong. In order to do this, he must conceive a separate class or "unique object" (the word "which is not like the others," "which does not get along with the others," "which is not of the same family").

Material

A sequence of four words is orally presented to the child. Three of these words belong to the same class (e.g., animals); the fourth does not belong; it is the "winner." Four series were devised, each comprised of twelve items, in which the common class was animals, parts of the body, dishes, and fruits and vegetables respectively. The fourth word, the word which did not belong to that class, could belong to a series other than the one in question.

The first item in each series are presented as examples:
1. duck, turkey, *bracelet,* chicken
2. Nose, mouth, ear, *bus*
3. *fox,* plate, glass, cup
4. apple, peach, *eye-glass,* pear

In designing the series, care was taken to: (1) choose simple words; (2) see that the words which did not fit or belong to that class did not form a homogeneous class by themselves, but rather that each of them was truly unique ("elephant," "swimmer," "staircase," "eye-glasses," "mountain," etc.); and (3) vary the position of the non-belonging words in the series to avoid answer sets.

Technique

The method of presentation was like that used in the test of perceptual contrast. The child is told that a set of four words will be read; in each set he must discover the "winner." There is one and only one "winner" in each set. Then the first set of Series I is read in a neutral voice. If the child immediately chooses the word that does not belong he is congratulated, and the experiment then proceeds to the next item. If he fails, he is told that he made a wrong choice and must choose another word. Then the four-word sequence is re-read. Note is made of the child's successive choices in getting the right answer. As soon as he selects the correct word the examiner proceeds to the next item. Thus, he finds out each time what the right answer is. After two or three items, the child is told there is a way or a "system" that makes it possible to know ahead of time which word is the winning one.

As in the perceptual task, a series was done successfully when the criterion of five consecutive correct answers was met: i.e., when the word which did not belong was selected on the first trial five times in a row. Then, whatever the outcome of the test once it was over, the child was asked to justify his choices. This made it possible for him to state a general classification law: "it's the word that doesn't go with the others," or "that's not the same kind," "that's different," etc.

Sample

Blind subjects: CA   8, N = 16
                       CA   9, N = 17
                       CA 10, N = 15

Sighted subjects: CA   6, N = 15
                     CA 7, N = 18
                     CA   8, N = 16
                     CA   9, N = 17

Results

1. *Median number of successful series.* Criterion was five successive correct answers regardless of the reason given by the subject for advancing them. Table 9 summarizes the median number of successful series for each age group of blind and sighted subjects.

Table 9
Median number of successfully completed series

CA	6	7	8	9	10
SV...	.44	1.83	3.30	3.82	
CB...			3.17	3.69	3.88

For blind and sighted children of the same age, none of the differences are significant (Median Test of Significance): i.e., the performance of the blind is equivalent to that of the sighted of the same age. These results are unlike those derived from the other tests; in preceding tests performance of the blind was inferior to that of the sighted, though differences varied from test to test.

2. *Subject's statement of general classificatory law.* The child was considered to have discovered the *general law* if his answer attended to the uniqueness of the object: "the one which is all alone," "the one which is not like the others," etc. Answers which only considered the aspect that applied in a particular instance were considered *partial discoveries:* "the one which is not an animal," "the one which is not a fruit," etc.

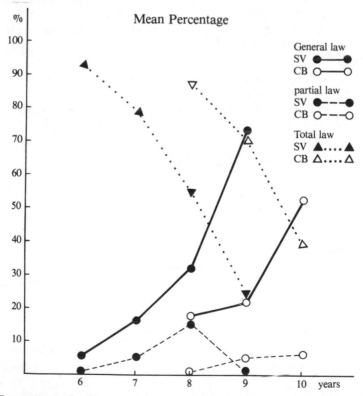

Fig. 20 Percentage of subjects who successfuly stated a general classification

Figure 20 indicates the percentage of subjects for each group and for each age who discovered the general law, the percentage who discovered the partial law, and the percentage who failed regardless of how many previous successes they had in selecting the words which did not belong in the various series. The data presented in Figure 20 demonstrate that the performance of the congenitally blind children is approximately one year below that of sighted subjects. At the age of nine, the difference between the two groups is significant at .01, but when the 10-year-old blind subjects are compared to nine-year-old sighted ones, differences are not significant (x^2).

3. *Correlation between the number of series successfully completed and the discovery of the law*: As with data derived from tests of perceptual contrast, the contingency coefficient was computed; the derived "r" was .47 for the congenitally blind group, and .50 for the sighted. Although both correlations are significant at the .001 level, they do not differ significantly.

4. *Comparison of CB and AB*: The same test was administered to a group of AB children, CA 8-10, and their performance was compared to that of a matched group of CB's which was randomly drawn from our total sample. The differences between these two groups were not significant in terms of the numbers of successful series not in terms of the discovery of the law (Sign Test and McNemar's Test).

Summary and Discussion

The most striking finding is that the performance of blind subjects generally approximates that of sighted children of the same age. This is still more remarkable when one considers previous findings regarding perceptual contrast. The principle and the structuring of the two types of test are very similar, as is the presentation of results. There are, however, three very important difference between them:

First, on the concrete task, the material used to elicit the child's reasoning, is *perceptually* oriented, whereas on the verbal task, emphasis is on the semantic meaning of the words. The second difference involves the very nature of the experimental material. In the perceptual task, the unique object is presented along with three other objects which are *identical* in all aspects; whereas in the verbal task, the unique object is presented with three words which are not identical but which, instead, *belong to the same class*. Clearly, the perceptual contrast is stronger than the verbal one. Finally, these two tasks have a different spatial-temporal quality. In the perceptual task, the four elements of each item are *simultaneously* present in the spatial field; while in the verbal task the four elements are read and, hence, are presented in *temporal* succession. Of course, a relationship is easier to apprehend when objects are presented simultaneously than when they are presented in succession; in the latter case one relies to some extent on the memory factor.

In summary, when one considers how the tasks are structured and presented, it is clear that discovery of the law based on perceptual contrast is less difficult than that based on semantic contrast; hence, more advances or elaborate intellectual processes must be brought to bear the latter.

The results presented in Figures 21 and 22 show striking differences in the performances of CB and SV subjects on these tasks.

Median Number of Series Successfully Completed

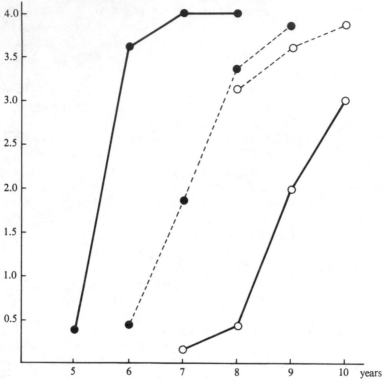

Fig. 21 Number of series successfully completed

Perceptive contrast		Semantic contrast	
SV ●－－●		SV ●——●	
CB ○－－○		CB ○——○	

1. *Comparison of results obtained from SV children.* Data presented in Figure 22 indicate the percentage of subjects who discovered the general law. The data serve to demonstrate that success on the perceptually-based task occurs much earlier than success on the verbally-based task. In view of the above-listed differences between the two tasks these results are not surprising. The contribution of concrete material in the discovery of the solution is evidenced by the differences in age at which successes are achieved. However, the early performance on perceptual tasks should be ascribed to perceptual intuition rather than to classificatory reasoning, per se.

2. *Comparison of results obtained from CB children.* Contrary to data obtained on SV subjects, the number of series successfully completed by the CB

subjects is *greater for the verbal than for the perceptual tasks*. Although differences in performance between the two tasks are less marked than are differences among the sighted subjects, they still are significant at .001 level. These findings indicate that at certain ages and in terms of the median number of successful series the verbal task is easier for the blind than the perceptive task. These differences are not maintained in data presented in Figure 22, which sets forth the percentage of subjects who discovered the general law. The two curves overlap; this indicates that the capacity to resolve the two problems appears simultaneously in the blind subjects.

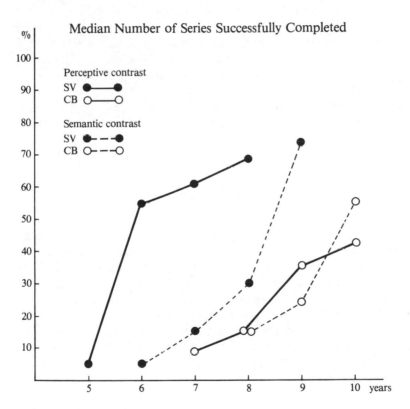

Fig. 22 Number of series successfully completed

In other words, one does not find among the blind the two- to three-year lag which marks the successful completion of the two tasks among the sighted. Around ages nine or 10, blind children find the solutions to the problem based on perceptual contrast and to the problem based on semantic contrast. The simultaneous emergence of these abilities among the blind, and the successive emergence among the sighted, explains why the performance of the blind on the verbal task is similar to that of the sighted, while the blind are seriously behind the sighted on the perceptual task.

Two tentative conclusions are drawn from these findings:

Logical reasoning, which is strongly influenced by verbal ability, develops normally in the blind, in spite of the major handicap they evidence in tasks of spatial and logical operations which involve concrete handling of objects.

On the other hand, the simultaneous success of the blind on the perceptual and verbal tasks provokes the hypothesis that, although in the sighted the psychological processes involved in these two tasks are different, they are analagous processes in the blind. The early success of the sighted on the perceptual task should be ascribed both to motor-perceptual organization and to cognitive processes. On the contrary, when the blind solve the perceptual task (which for them is difficult) they make use of more elaborate symbolic and logical processes, and thus compensate for their insufficient motor-perceptual (tactual) organization. The emergence of these symbolic and logical processes around ages nine or ten could account for their delayed success with the perceptual task and their contemporaneous success with the verbal task.

In the succeeding paragraphs there will be a review of our remaining research on the development of verbally-based operations among blind subjects. After presentation of these results it will be possible to consider the over-all problem of the development of intellectual operations in blind children.

Class Inclusion and Quantification of Inclusion

Ordering within a class by blind subjects is interesting for two reasons. On a theoretical plane consideration is addressed to a basic operation which leads to the bidirectional handling of mutually articulated concepts: (1) placing each class in turn in a progressively more inclusive one, or *ascending order;* and (2) progressively differentiating each class into sub-classes and these into further sub-classes, or *descending order.* This study has a practical advantage; it requires little concrete equipment. The essentials of the problem can be presented orally as questions and answers.

What is meant by quantification of inclusion (Piaget and Inhelder, 1959)? Let us suppose there is a class A, and another class B included in A in such a way that $A = B + B^1$ (where B^1, the complementary class to B, is different from zero). The operation of quantification of inclusion consists of comparing A and B from the standpoint of extension: i.e., deducing that if $A = B + B^1$, then $B = A - B^1$, hence B is smaller than A. For example, the class "flowers" is larger, in extension, than the included class "daisies".

Mastering this apparently very simple problem, however, requires a long period of elaboration, and generally is accomplished by children at ages eight or nine. In order to handle these ordered classes correctly, the child must first be able to move from the direct operation of addition, which characterizes the relation $A = B + B^1$ (flowers = daisies plus non-daisies), to the reverse operation $B = A - B^1$ (daisies = flowers minus non-daisies). The reversal process, it is known, occurs only at the operatory level. Furthermore, in comparing the parts of the whole, the child must keep track of the particular properties of the whole and its unity; this generally is not achieved before age eight either. Thus, if one shows the child a bunch of flowers comprised of two roses and eight daisies, the most characteristic error of young children consists in maintaining that there are more daisies than flowers in the bunch, even though they have asserted that both roses and daisies are flowers (Piaget and Inhelder, 1959, p. 104).

The reason for this error is quite clear. At this level, the child is quite capable of deciding whether a certain part belongs to the whole: i.e., of subsuming the two sub-classes, roses and daisies, under the class flowers. But when questioned about the relative extension of flowers and daisies the child cannot reason simultaneously about the part (daisies) and the whole (flowers) because the latter is made up of the sum of two or more parts (roses + daisies + etc.). He limits himself to comparison of the extension of the two sub-classes under consideration, to the comparison of the two parts themselves. Thus he maintained that there are more daisies than flowers "because there are eight daisies and two roses." Typically, subjects at the pre-operational level find it difficult to conserve the whole class, to consider it as the sum of the sub-classes or parts, and to treat these sub-classes as parts which comprise the whole.

Even though the verbal base is obvious in this type of task, the problems encountered by the child cannot be regarded as sheer linguistic obstacles. Generally, a child's language construction is accomplished between ages two and four. This accomplishment allows the naming of animals, birds, flowers, etc., long before categories are subsumed one within another: e.g., "dogs" within "animals."

Comparison of blind and sighted children is a simple problem. The blind, like the sighted, possess the linguistic structures inherent in language. Here, only a minor role is played by the representation and concrete handling of objects involved in logical reasoning. Under these circumstances, will the blind again perform in an inferior manner? Or will they master the operation of reversibility (an operation which is basic to the ordering of classes) at the same age as the sighted? In view of our original hypothesis, performance of the blind is expected to be equivalent to that of the sighted, since these tasks do not involve a strong concrete base.

Materials and techniques

The experimental material consists of a "bouquet" of six artificial flowers: i.e., four daisies and two roses. After the material is displayed, the child is reminded that on the table there are four daisies and two roses. Next he is asked if daisies are flowers and if roses are flowers also (these questions always get an affirmative answer). Then the roses and daisies are combined in one single bouquet and the Piaget-Inhelder question is posed:

1. "Are there more flowers or more daisies on the table? Why?" The next two questions are designed to make the situation more concrete, and thereby help the child reason in terms of mutually inclusive classes:

2. "Suppose you make a bouquet, using *all the flowers* on the table; then you put them back on the table. Next, I make a bouquet, using *all the daisies* on the table. Who will have made the bigger bouquet, you or I? Why?"

3. "If I take all the flowers that are on the table, will there be any daisies left on the table, and if I take all the daisies that are on the table will there be any flowers left on the table?" Then Question 1 is repeated because it is the basic question.

4. "Are there more flowers or more daisies on the table? Why?"

During this portion of the test, the bouquet remains in front of the child who is reminded frequently that it is made up of four daisies and two roses, and also reminded that "daisies are flowers, and so are roses." Finally, the bouquet is removed and the child is asked a last question, one which extends the problem to flowers that are not present.

5. "If somebody said: 'I would like to count all the flowers there are in all the gardens of the world'; and then somebody else said: 'I would like to count all the daisies in all the gardens of the world'; who will have more to count: the one who wants to count all the flowers in the world, or the one who wants to count all the daisies in the world? Why?"

Note that the action referred to in the present experiment is "counting" the flowers, whereas Piaget and Inhelder referred to "picking" them. The substitutions was made in the belief that children would regard "picking" as a material impossibility; a "cut" or "picked" flower is destroyed. The person who picked "all the flowers in the world" would "leave nothing" for the one who came afterwards and wished to pick all the daisies. However, to the child, the act of simply "counting" all the flowers leaves them intact for the next person who wishes to "count" all the daisies.

Sample

Congenitally blind subjects: CA 8-9, N = 12
                                CA 10,   N = 10
                                CA 11,   N = 13

Sighted subjects: CA 7,   N = 40
                                CA 8,   N = 40
                                CA 9,   N = 32
                                CA 10,   N = 21

Results

Because the answers to Question 1 tend to reflect the child's confusion over the new and unexpected problem they will not be analyzed now. Instead, there will be a review of answers to Question 4. The intervening Questions 2 and 3 have provided the child with practice and clarification; therefore, Question 4 tends to be answered more successfully than Question 1. Because Questions 2 and 3 are answered satisfactorily by both blind and sighted children in the age range included in the study they actually serve as openers. For these reasons, analysis centers on answers to Questions 4 (inclusion when material is immediately perceptible) and Question 5 (general inclusion).

1. *Quantification of inclusion–concrete material* (Question 4). Figure 23 indicates the percentage of children, sighted and congenitally blind, by age groups, who correctly answered this question. The success curve for the blind approxi-

mates that of sighted, especially at ages eight and nine. At age 10, however, blind children appeared slightly inferior to sighted ones. Because of the small number of subjects in this age group it is impossible to apply a test of significance, but if the 10- and 11-year-old blind subjects are combined and then compared with the 10-year-old sighted ones, differences are not significant (X^2). Also, there is *no* difference between 10-year-old sighted subjects and 11-year-old blind ones.

It is concluded that the performance of blind children approximates that of the sighted, and when a deficit exists it does not exceed one year.

2. *Quantification of inclusion—non-perceptual material* (Question 5). One could expect that children would find it more difficult to quantify inclusion when the questions involved concepts such as "all the flowers in the world" and "all the daisies in the whole world" than when the questioning involved concrete objects. If the child is presented a bouquet, he can easily count the number of flowers (6) and the number of daisies (4), and immediately note the difference. Obviously, this cannot be done when he has to deal with "all the flowers in the whole world."

Surprisingly, the percentage of successes in answer to the verbal concept exceeded the percentage of successful answers to Question 4, although the bouquet was present when Question 4 was administered. These findings, which are set forth in Figure 24, apply to the various age groups of both blind and sighted subjects.

Later analysis of reasons given for the answers did not confirm these successes. Often the justification given by the subjects was, "There are many kinds of flowers (tulips, roses, violets, etc.), whereas there is only one kind of daisy." When a child advances this type of reasoning, it is impossible to determine if he has achieved the notion of greater class extension in flowers as compared to daisies because flowers = daisies + non-daisies (which is true inclusion), or if he simply reached his conclusion by comparing the sub-class of daisies to a sub-class of non-daisies made up of roses + tulips + violets + etc. In the latter case, the child is comparing only two parts of the whole (daisies and non-daisies), not a part with the whole which includes it (flowers and daisies).

For clarification of Question 5 the following sub-question was added:

5a. "If someone counted all the flowers in the whole world, would he also count daisies?"

A large number of sighted children, CA 7 and 8, and of blind children, CA 8-9, answered this question negatively. Therefore, their success in answering Question 5 is not indicative of concept attainment. In the thought of young children, the person who "counts all flowers" actually counts all flowers except daisies.

Thus Question 5a. is crucial in determining the children's understanding. Unfortunately, it was included only after some data had been collected. Hence, Figure 24 reflects answers to Question 5 as it was originally asked. The fact that Question 5 was answered correctly more often than Question 4 derives from the ambiguous nature of Question 5. In any case, when answers given by the various groups of blind and sighted subjects are compared, there are no differences among them; performances are similar in all respects.

3. *Comparison between CB and AB.* The group of adventitiously blind children was composed of only seven children, ages eight to eleven. No differences were found between the matched group of CB and AB. But, as happened in another experiment, one reason for the lack of discrimination between the two groups was that both groups had near optimum performance.

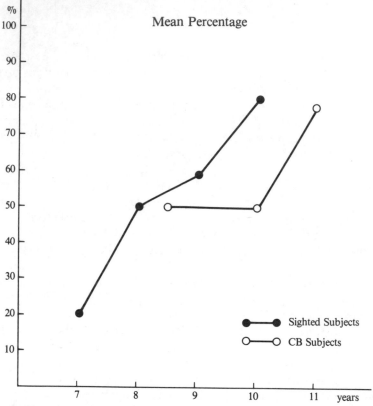

Fig. 23 Percentage of subjects who achieved quantification of inclusion on concrete material (Question 4).

Conclusions

In summary, as a whole, these data serve to demonstrate that when blind and sighted children are asked to reason about "abstract" categories, without recourse to concrete material, which is more or less structured on the perceptual plane, they behave in the same or like manner. Similar findings evolved from the previous test which required discovery of a law based on verbal contrast.

Interest in these results is heightened when it is recalled that in the attempt to classify geometric forms along one, two, or three criteria, the blind perform much more poorly than sighted subjects. Again, there emerges simultaneously in the blind the abilities to deal with perceptual and with verbal contrast, whereas among sighted subjects, and due to their experiences with concrete materials, these emerge one after the other.

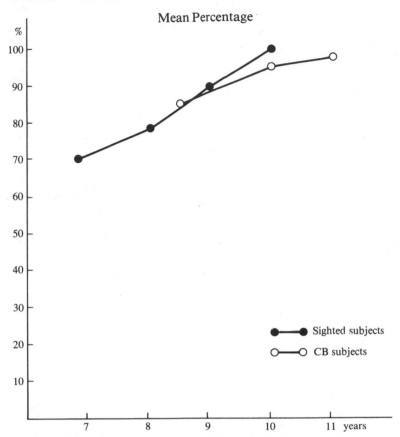

Fig. 24 Percentage of subjects who achieved quantification of inclusion on non-perceptible material.

Seriation

Just as there was an attempt to find classification tasks which were not based on the perception of concrete objects, so was there interest in results obtained when blind and sighted subjects seriated, not concrete, manipulable objects, but objects which were verbally described.

To achieve this, one of Burt's 1919 problems in verbal seriation was selected. It was the one used by Piaget in his 1921 and 1924 research. In principle, the subject is given three elements, related two by two in terms of size or color, etc. The task is to deduce, through transitivity, the relation which links any one of these elements to any other. Burt gave the now famous example: "Edith is fairer than Susan, but Edith is darker than Lili. Which one of the three is darkest?" In formal terms the problem can be written:

A (Edith) > B (Susan; and
A (Edith) < C (Lili).
(the signs > and < meaning lighter and darker, respectively)

One then gets the relationship

B < A < C

From this relationship it is easy to conclude that B is the < of all:

i.e., Susan is the darkest of the three.

The fact that young children cannot carry out this type of ordering is demonstrated by Burt's original work, as well as by Piaget's (1921) later study (which in 1924 was integrated into his general theory of children's logic). Below a certain level of development, children's comparisons lacked completion and order; most often they conceived of color in absolute ("Edith is blonde," "Lili is a brunette") rather than in relative terms (even though the suggestion of relativity implied in the words "more" and "less" indicate that multiple intermediaries existed.

Hunter (1957a) systematically studied the answers of children and adolescents to such a problem. Rather than maintaining Burt's and Piaget's use of "fairer" and "darker" ("more blond" and "more brunette"), he used the relationship of size ("bigger" and "smaller" which can easily be represented mentally) and the relationship "happier" and "sadder" which involved an abstract affective response (Hunter, 1957a). A single problem of the type: "If A > B and B > C, which is the biggest? Which is the smallest?" was presented by him under the eight possible formulations, namely:

if A > B > C, which is >?
if A > B > C, which is <?
if A > B, and C < B, which is >?
if B < A, and B > C, which is >?

Responses from subjects, ages 11 and 16, provided Hunter with the following conclusions: (1) the various formulations are not equally difficult: the easiest ones are those of the type A > B > C, and the hardest ones are those of the type B < A, B > C, which demand a more complex reordering. Nevertheless, this gradation in difficulty is more obvious in the responses of the 16-year-old subjects than in the responses of the 11-year-olds; (2) young children are more sensitive to "contextual factors" than older ones; (3) 11-year-old children resolve the problems of size more easily than those of affect or mood; this difference is not maintained in subjects aged 16 years; and, finally, (4) the 16-year old subjects are more apt to profit from practicing the test.

Hunter concludes that as they grow older, people become progressively more capable of manipulating the logical structure which underlies the series, thereby freeing themselves both from the individual content of each problem and from the contextual factors which engender faulty answers.

Interest in this type of problem is understandable. The way in which blind and sighted children succeed in ordering concrete objects has been analyzed, and particularly their ability to insert a new object in an already ordered series. Burt's problem is based on the same logical structures as are the problems of concrete seriations, except that Burt's seriations problem is posed verbally, with no reference to readily perceivable real objects or individuals. Piaget (1960), using Burt's original formulations, found that this makes the problem more difficult than the preceding ones, so much more, in fact, that it generally is not solved until the ages of 11 to 12: i.e., at the beginning of the formal stage.

Because of these circumstances, there is the desire to determine how blind children (who are seriously handicapped in the ordering of cubes and sticks, but not so handicapped in the ordering of weights) will perform when the task involves verbal logic. The study of verbal seriation serves to eliminate or reduce the help derived from actually perceiving the structure of the elements. Thus, the general hypothesis will be tested: blind and sighted subjects display a similar behavior when their reasoning involves only verbal propositions.

Material

Since Burt's formulation of the problem involved color it was not suitable for blind subjects. Instead, Hunter's problem involving the relation of size was selected. All children, even the blind, have everyday personal experience with size.

Instead of following Hunter's method of presenting the same problem under eight different guises, we presented problems which were simpler in structure, and hence easier to solve: i.e., problems adapted for use with our nine- to ten-year-old subjects. Seven problems were retained which were similar in type to: "John is taller than Peter, Peter is taller than Robert; which one of the three is the tallest?"

1. $A > B$, $B > C$; which one is $>$? (A)
2. $A > B$, $B > C$; which one is $<$? (C)
3. $A > B$, $B < C$; which one is $<$? (B)
4. $A < B$, $B > C$; which one is $>$? (B)
5. $A = B$, $C > B$; which one is $>$? (C)
6. $A > B$, $C > B$; which one is $<$? (B)
7. $A = B$, $C < A$; is $B >$ or $< C$? ($>$)

Each of the seven problems was presented twice (but not in succession) using different children's names; therefore, there were 14 answers per subject.

Technique

Two modes of presentation were selected and applied to alternate groups:

Oral presentation. Each problem was read to the child, slowly and with emphasis on the different terms in the relation. The statement was read again as often as necessary with no time limit.

Written presentation. Each problem was presented to the child, in writing, on a card; the child first read the text aloud, then he gave his answer; again there was no time limit.

Sample

The test was administered to two groups of sighted children. One group was presented the oral form; the other the written. Blind children were given only the oral version of the test for two reasons: (1) not all eight- and nine-year-old blind children read Braille; (2) the number of blind subjects was not sufficient to permit division into two different groups.

The number and ages of subjects administered the oral and written versions are presented in Table 10.

Table 10
Number of blind and sighted subjects given oral and written forms of the verbal seriation test

Ages	Oral Version		Written Version
	SV	CB	SV
8 years	20	9	18
9 years	18	13	17
10 years	25	18	

Table 11.
Mean number of successful answers (Maximum = 14)

Ages	Oral Version		Written Version
	SV	CB	SV
8 years	8.33	11.25	9.00
9 years	10.00	11.75	10.88
10 years	11.41	11.75	

Results

The small sample size did not permit the desired grouping of the subjects. Hence, it is not possible to study separately the relative difficulty of each problem; instead, there will be a comparison of the results obtained by the various groups of subjects.

The mean scores of successes for each age was computed and the distribution of scores set forth in Table 11.

Oral presentation

The performance of blind children is superior to that of sighted ones. Differences, however, are significant only for age eight (P = .01, Mann-Whitney U-Test). It is the first time in the entire study that such differences have occurred. On previous measures, the blind either were inferior or at best equal to the sighted. Now, superiority of the blind at age eight raises a technical question. During test administration it was noted that sighted subjects experienced a great deal of difficulty remembering the problems; generally, several readings were necessary. On the contrary, blind children were completely at ease with this kind of presentation, and tended to answer correctly after hearing the problem only one or two times. These differences in behavior are understandable: sighted children, age eight, have received only a limited amount of training in oral exercises (or, as the French term it, "mental calculus") at ages eight and nine, most of their school exercises are presented in writing. By contrast and because the Braille system is both difficult and limited, teachers for the blind rely heavily on oral instructions. Also, young blind children listen to the radio, records, etc., rather than read books. These experiences promote development of a powerful auditory memory.

To determine if the superiority of the blind over the sighted could be attributed to the sighted's poor auditory memory a second set of sighted subjects was presented the written version of the test: i.e., a method of presentation commonly encountered by them.

Written presentation

Two remarks are made concerning the results set forth in Table 11, for sighted subjects on the written version of the test.

First, although not statistically significant (Mann-Whitney U-Test), their performance is improved.

Second, in spite of this improvement, their performance, particularly at age eight, is poorer than that of the blind. At age eight, differences between scores for the blind on oral presentation and scores for the sighted on written presentation, are significant at .001 level. At age nine, the blind and sighted children have similar scores.

Even though the written presentation is, in a sense, more concrete, and does eliminate the problem of oral memory for the sighted, their performance still does not equal that of the blind.

"Contextual factors"

These are factors which are derived from the text of the statement, and which unduly influence the right answer or the wrong answer. For cxample, in the problem:

A > B, B < C; which one is < ?

the child, without any logical reflection, may tend to answer "B" simply because the question ("which one is the smallest?") repeats the second part of the statement of the problem ("B is smaller than C"). In such a case, contextual bias is in terms of the right answer. On the contrary, in the problem:

A < B, B > C; which one is < ?

no such bias can occur.

When the seven problems used in the present study were analyzed, it appeared that contextual factors may have influenced the child's answers to problems 3, 4, and 5; but not to problems 2, 6, and 7. Could it be that the equal or superior performance of the blind derived from the fact that they were more sensitive to these factors? To answer this, separate examination was accorded the results obtained for problems:

3. A>B, B<C; which one is <? (B)
4. A<B, B>C; which one is >? (B)
5. A = B, C>B; which one is >? (C)

and, on the other hand, for problems:

2. A>B, B>C; which one is <? (C)
6. A>B, C>B; which one is <? (B)
7. A = B, C<A; is B> or <C? (>)

The mean number of successes (maximum = 6) achieved by blind and sighted subjects for each of the sub-categories appear in Tables 12 and 13.

Table 12

Mean number of successful answers to the three problems which contain contextual bias

Ages	Oral Version			Written Version
	SV		CB	SV
8 years	4.33	p = .05	4.60	p = .02	3.67
9 years	4.11	←——→	5.77	←——→	5.40

Table 13

Mean number of successful answers to the three problems which do not contain contextual bias

Ages	Oral Version			Written Version
	SV		CB	SV
8 years	3.50	p = .05	5.60	4.78
9 years	4.50	←——→	5.00	

1. *Problems with contextual bias.* At age nine, differences between blind and sighted subjects are not significant. But at age eight, differences between CB and SV (oral version) are significant at the .05 level. Likewise, the differences between CB and SV (written version) are significant at the .02 level. Among the sighted subjects, there is no difference between the two kinds of presentation.

2. *Problems without contextual bias.* Again, differences are not significant at age nine. At age eight, the performance of the blind on the oral version is significantly superior to that of the sighted (.05 level). However, differences are not significant between CB and SV on the written version.

Thus, performance of the blind remains either slightly superior or equal to that of the sighted, regardless of whether the sighted are provided the oral or written version of the questions.

Conclusions

Success of the blind on these problems is surprising when one remembers that at the same ages they did not experience equivalent success on reasoning problems which involved concrete objects. For instance, they had difficulty in discovering a law based on a perceptual contrast, in classifying geometrical forms, and in ordering cubes and sticks. The paradoxical fact is that solutions to purely verbal tests are more easily achieved by the blind than solutions to concrete tests of equivalent logical structure. This data contradicts findings about the reasoning of the child, findings which have been verified time and again.

Chapter Seven

CONCLUSIONS

Initial discussion centers on the characteristics of functional development of the blind child, as identified in the present study.

Characteristics of Functional Development of the Congenitally Blind

The experimental results discussed in the preceding chapters are recapitulated in Figure 25. Order of presentation for the experimental situations is (1) "infra-logical" (spatial and physical) operations which tend to construct the object, and (2) "logical" operations which establish relations between given objects. The logical operations are subdivided in terms of operations which are based on concrete handling and operations with a verbal base. Against these is plotted the "mean" age at which each specific test was successfully performed by 55 percent of the subjects. Although the data are approximate — i.e., there is no uniform scoring because different scoring systems were applied to various measures — they do serve to indicate the main characteristics of logical development in the congenitally blind and in the sighted.

In the graph a solid line represents the time-lag between achievement by blind and sighted subjects. The inferiority of the blind is extreme at the left of the graph (infralogical tasks), but decreases in the right person (verbal-logial tasks). This decrease was hypothesized.

Preliminary Remarks

Interpretation of findings will be preceded by a discussion of uncontrolled factors which may have influenced these results.

First, all tasks are based on concrete material and involve actual handling of objects. Because of the *motor handicap* generally displayed by blind children precautions were taken to control for the effects of this deficiency when designing and when *administering each test*. Nonetheless, the possibility of confounding effects due to a motor difficulty must be considered.

Second, in academic areas at the elementary school level, blind children, when compared to sighted children, show an average time-lag of three years. Is this delay responsible for their intellectual performance? Answer to the question is needed if valid interpretation of our experimental results is to be achieved.

Third, the presentation of concrete material involved in spatial, physical, and certain figurative tasks is done *simultaneously*, while the presentation of verbal material involved in other tasks is done *successively*. The effect of this variation also should be investigated.

Motor Deficiency

Perceptual apprehension of outside reality is accomplished by the blind through tactual channels. The exploratory movements which characterize this sensory modality are important because they enlarge the perceptual field. In fact, in the tactile domain, "perceptual activity" can hardly be dissociated from general sensory-motor activity: i.e., it is the general motor capabilities which contribute to tactile perception, while in vision only ocular motor ability is employed. Thus it seems necessary to establish stages of motor development characteristic of blind children, and also to analyze, within Piaget's theoretical framework, the relations between motor development, perception, and operations.

Often the term "motor development" is loosely used. Psychological reviews covering the subject are few. Generally, research reflects professional selection: e.g., conditions are sought which permit the blind labor force to compete with the sighted without distinguishing between congenitally and adventitiously blind subjects, or even partially and totally blind persons. Although genetic studies are extremely rare, research by Norris, Brodie, and Spaulding (1957) has established that the psychomotor development of blind infants is comparable to that of sighted infants except in tasks where fine motor coordination is required (e.g., pegboard), and in the age at which the child first walks. Average age for the blind to walk alone is between 15 months and three to four years. The delay may, perhaps, result from attitudes of overprotective parents who, because of fear of "accidents," surround the child with "don'ts." These prohibitions create feelings of insecurity within the child; in turn, the insecurity generates various types of motor inhibitions.

The speed and precision with which the congenitally blind performed motor tasks were found to be significantly inferior to those of the adventitiously blind subjects; similarly, totally blind subjects were inferior to the partially blind (Bauman, 1946; Buell, 1950). These results were not unexpected: the role of sight in the orientation of gesture and in the organization of the field of action seemed obvious; there is no doubt that deprivation of sight deeply affects motor efficiency.

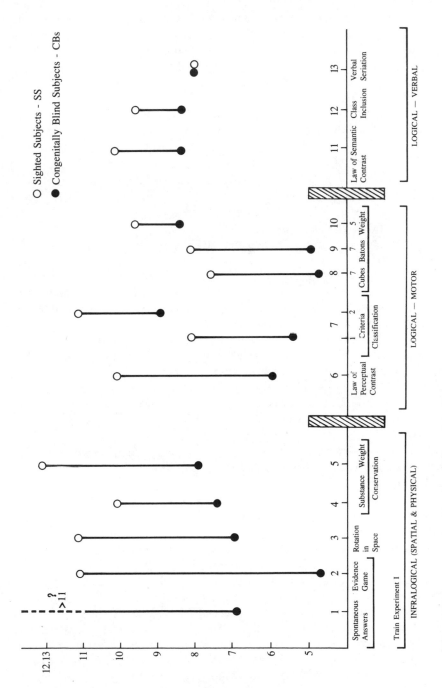

Fig. 25 Mean age of achieving different tasks.

The quantitative aspect of motor efficiency, however, is not a main concern. The main interest lies in the influence of primary disorders on the coordination of movements or gestures oriented toward a specific action. Because systematic research is totally lacking on this subject, one must rely on the clinical observations of physicians, psychologists, and educators who work with blind children. These workers report frequent psychomotor difficulties in blind children: e.g., stiffness of movements, poor coordination, etc. (Lairy, Netchine and Neyrault, 1962).

Does the presence of motor disorders hinder the development of logical operations? Piaget posits that motor activity plays an essential role in the development of operations. When he speaks of sensory-motor activity, the sensory element is only the "signifier"; by contrast, the "signified" has an active motor origin. He writes, characteristically: "All cognitive mechanisms rest on motor activity. . . . Acquisition of knowledge is foremost an action by the subject on the object, and therefore it implies a basic and *permanent motor dimension* which remains present at more advanced levels" (Piaget, 1956).

By motor activity, Piaget does not mean the motor act viewed in terms of its precision, rapidity, coordination, etc., but rather the act in its wholeness: i.e., the actions themselves, "which are not any movements, but systems of movements coordinated as a function of some result or intention" (1960). This "permanent motor dimension," which, according to Piaget, would be present at all developmental levels, is nothing but the coordination of sensory-motor schemes.

There is still need, however, to determine the relations which exist between this progressive coordination of schemes (which Piaget views as basic to the development of operations) and the development of the child's motor capacities. Answers to the questions will emerge from a discussion of data obtained from psychotherapy and from animal experimentation, as well as from certain findings from our own experiments.

1. *Psychopathology*: The intellectual development of post-polio children whose paralysis was peripheral and from medullary origin, was studied by Grossiord (1961). The conclusion derived from the study was that paralysis of this type did not affect intellectual functioning.

In another study, the Terman, the Kohs, and the Porteus tests were administered to 76 post-polio subjects, ages five to 12, by Rossi (1961) who found that a slight inferiority, which existed only on the Terman performance, could be attributed to a lack of social experiences. This lack was attributed to early hospitalization rather than to motor incapacity itself.

Apraxia is a different disease implying a central disorganization of goal-oriented actions. Piaget (1960) has asked if apraxia disturbs the operations themselves or if it disturbs the figurative aspects of symbolization. Although a study by Stambak (1964) on childhood dyspraxia is not conclusive in its determination of the processes affected, it does point to behavioral effects which are similar to those observed in blind children. It seems that the determining factor lies in the insufficiency of figurative rather than motor organizations.

2. *Animal experimentation*: Forgays and Forgays (1952) raised rats in small circular cages which limited their motor activity, but which offered a great variety of visual stimulation. A second group of rats, matched to the first, was placed in the inverse situation: they moved freely in much larger cages, but had no visual stimulation: i.e., they were kept in constant darkness. A third control group was raised in normal conditions which allowed both motor activity and visual stimulation. All three groups were then administered a maze learning test. The results imply that in even a relatively simple maze-learning experiment, the effects of visual deprivation are much more acute than those of motor deprivation. Confirming results were obtained by Hymovitch (1952).

3. Data from an experiment by Axelrod (1959; which provides evidence of lowered performance by blind children on an oral test which required discovery of a law) suggest that factors other than motor are required to account for poorer performance on various logical tests.

4. Findings from the present study indicate:

First, although the amount of motor exploration is identical, the blind perform more poorly on spatial and physical tasks than on concrete logical ones (classification, seriation). Furthermore, motor difficulties do not explain the extreme time-lag evidenced by the blind in conservation of weight while their performance approximates that of the sighted on seriation of weights.

Second, performance of congenitally blind subjects, whose loss of vision is attributed to retrolental fibroplasia, demonstrates that children in this group frequently experience such motor deficiencies as lack of coordination, poor muscle tone, lack of stamina, etc., which generally occur in conjunction with prematurity (Parmelee, 1959). Yet when, in the present study, their performance was compared to that of a matched group of blind of other etiologies the differences between the two groups were not significant even in spatial tasks.

Although a definitive answer still is lacking, data indicate that motor disorders observed among blind children cannot account solely for their characteristic operatory development.

Lag in school achievement

Causes for this academic lag fall into three general categories:

1. delayed school entrance due to geographical distribution which necessitates boarding-school accommodations;

2. irregular attendance due to general health conditons and to surgical interventions;

3. slower rate of progression through grade levels by the blind.

The first two categories are exogenous, while the third one relates to the situation generated by blindness.

When, one by one, the total sample of blind subjects was reviewed, the importance of each of these factors for each child and for each group became apparent. The second category was controlled; one of our criteria for selection of subjects was uninterrupted school attendance. Also, most surgical intervention occurs at an age much younger than that of our subjects. It is the adventitiously blind children, rather than the congenitally blind, whose absenteeism can be attributed to receipt of medical services.

Out of the 86 subjects constituting the total congenitally blind sample, 49 percent attended kindergarten—i.e., were registered in school before age seven; 78 percent before age eight; and only 22 percent entered school between ages eight and nine. From these figures, it is clear that delayed school entrance alone cannot justify age advance without grade advance.

In fact, the determining factor seems to be the third category. The demands of the Braille graphic system are not the only contributors to this slower rate of progression. An alternative viewpoint would attribute the delayed progression to the late appearance of the logical structures basic to progression in learning. This implies that school exercises do not accelerate the formation of these structures. Educators have long known that such academic exercises are ineffective if applied prematurely. A commensurate level of development must be achieved by the child if he is to be receptive to notions transmitted in school.

The time-lag in the blind for the development of successful responses in our research varies from a maximum of four to five years in some areas to a negligible minimum in verbal seriation. Thus, the two or three years of academic delay actually observed in the blind may represent an approximate average figure of their cognitive capabilities.

Simultaneous and Successive Character of Perceptual "Givens"

Figure 25 shows that the performances of the blind are near those of the sighted in the tasks implying a successive presentation of the data (weight seriation and verbal logical tasks). Can the temporal nature of the subjects' apprehension of these experimental materials account for the trend reflected in the data? Blind subjects may be more successful in tasks which involve successive apprehension (which characterizes tactual perception), while the performance of sighted subjects fails to maintain the superiority these subjects demonstrate in situations which permit simultaneous visual perception of materials.

To answer the above question, it would have been necessary to include tests which assess temporal operations in the blind as well as measures of logical operations based on successive auditory stimuli. A comparative study of spatial and temporal operations would have established ages for successful achievement and would have indicated the level and type of difficulties encountered by blind children. Both areas are considered by Piaget as being within the framework of infralogical operations. For this reason, it would have been particularly helpful to determine on which measures blind children's performances differ from those of the sighted. The information also would be helpful in determining relationships between successive auditory and tactual stimuli. The fact that such studies are not included in this research constitutes an essential weakness.

Although not solutions to the problem, certain points can be reviewed which emphasize the importance of this factor in the general interpretation of the results.

One aspect which contributed to the difficulty of the temporal succession tasks —i.e., the mnemonic organization of the "data"—was partially controlled in at least one of the experiments. In tasks of verbal seriations, it is possible that the difficulties exhibited by the eight- to nine-year-old sighted subjects (their ability to integrate long verbal statements) stemmed from their lack of experience with verbal exercises. By contrast, the techniques used in schools for the blind, which include extensive use of oral instruction and of memorization of texts, prepare these children for this task. In a second step there was an attempt to control the influence of memory; the performance of blind children on orally presented problems was compared to that of sighted subjects who were presented the same problems, but in written form. Although the sighted subjects' performance improved when this technique was employed, it did not surpass that of the blind: i.e., difficulties encountered by sighted subjects on a verbal seriation task are not due exclusively to the mode of presentation, successive oral or written, but to the logical structure involved in the problem.

The goal of Axelrod's (1959) research was to show that (contrary to what generally was sustained in psychological literature) the congenitally blind's deficiency was not limited to the spatial domain nor to insufficiency in "visualization" (Worchel, 1951), but rather that their handicap also was evident in conceptual activities which did not involve visualization: e.g., tactual classification and generalization of a law from the tactual to the auditory domain and vice versa.

To assess his ability to generalize, the subject was presented with three stimuli: two identical and one observably different. One of the two identical stimuli was always placed in the intermediary position, while the other came either before or after. The rewarded stimulus was always the one of the two identical ones not in the central position, and the subject had to discover that law. This experimental design was applied to both tactual stimuli (geometric forms) and auditory ones (sounds of a different timbre). By alternately opening the session with tactual and auditory tasks, Axelrod sought to determine if the possibility for generalization was comparable among congenitally blind and sighted subjects. His results show that the blind were systematically inferior to the sighted in this domain. But if only the auditory task was considered, and considered only when it was given first—i.e., independent of any phenomenon of generalization or transfer—the percentage of correct answers given by the sighted was significantly superior to that of the blind. In other words, even in a task involving successively-presented auditory stimuli, the blind's performance was inferior to that of the sighted. Also, use of analysis of variance techniques did not result in significant difference between the auditory and the tactual tests: i.e., for the blind, the auditory task was not easier than the tactual one.

Although these findings were of interest, they could not be directly integrated into the framework of our results. Axelrod's study was not genetic, and although his subjects' ages varied from nine to 18, his computations were divided not by age groups but by a total grouping of 82 subjects.

One cannot deny the possible influence of a "temporal factor" (simultaneity versus successiveness) as well as a "spatial factor" (concrete objects versus abstract concepts) on the performance of both blind and sighted subjects. However, rather than making them basic to the interpretation of present results, observed facts will be analyzed in an effort to determine what could be responsible for the difficulties of the blind in arriving at the notion of space as well as other concepts concerned with the world of real objects. Then there will be discussion of the interpretation of insufficiences in a certain form of perceptual apprehension which are due to deprivation of sight, and which are common sources of difficulties in logical reasoning observed in blind children.

Principal Aspects of the Development of Logic in the Blind

In summary, these results indicate that the essential consequence of the deprivation of sight is a disturbance in the notion of space, and the earlier the onset of blindness the more severe is this deficiency. On this point, present results support various studies cited in Chapter 1. While deprived of the vast visual perceptual field, and of the multiple simultaneous perceptions it is capable of transmitting, the blind child also is deprived of the elementary spatial representations which, when progressively ordered and coordinated, enable him to construct a coherent object. Thus, primitive spatial relations—e.g., the front and the rear of a moving train, or a dog running behind a truck, etc.—are not clearly established in the blind child's mind until the approximate age of 10. By contrast, the sighted child is able, as early as three to four years of age, to organize these different relations in one logic system.

Certainly the present study has not investigated all the operations constituting the notion of space. To do so it would have been necessary to supplement the study of displacement with others concerned with elaborations of the notion of space: e.g., the constitution of the notion of coordinates (vertical and horizontal) or the notion of measurement. However, within our limited framework the findings are sufficiently explicit to permit the conclusion: early impoverishment of perceptual experiences due to visual deprivation is followed by an important delay in the constitution of spatial operations. This delay demonstrated the close ties which, at the initial stages of the construction of the notion of space, exists between perceptual (or Piagetian "figurative") aspects and imagery, on the one hand, and the logical and rational aspects (operative) on the other hand: i.e., any damage to the inferior level has repercussions at the superior level.*

Deprivation of sight is not only a disturbance of the notion of space. Indeed, findings provide evidence of a systematic inferiority of the congenitally blind in physical operations which involve conservation and in concrete logical operations which involve forms of classifications and seriations.

According to Piaget, notions of invariance are basic to the act of knowing, and constitute a most telling example of the reversible character of intellectual operations. A delay of two-to-three years appeared in the acquisition of the notion of conservation by the blind child: i.e., the logical composition of actions involving sectioning, lengthening, displacement, etc., is possible for him only after the age of 10. The delay is significant because conservation of quantities often is considered as

---

* It would also be interesting to analyze where damage to the operational level is followed inversely by modifications at the figurative level. A study of perceptual structures and of imagery in the mentally retarded would accomplish this.

a typical case of conflict between perceptual data and reasoning; the true role of reasoning goes beyond the immediate transformation, to reconstitute the "history" of it. The difficulties of the congenitally blind, as well as the superiorities of the adventititously blind, indicate that impoverishment of general perceptual experiences, far from attenuating such a conflict, continue it by partially depriving the individual of means which could aid in its resolution.

In the conservation of weight task, performance of the blind was expected to be identical to that of the sighted; however, diametrically opposed results were obtained: not only did the blind perform less well, but their time-lag was more accentuated in this than in conservation of substance tasks. This paradoxical finding is explained in part by the fact that, when placed in a situation of equal logical difficulty, blind and sighted children do not have use of the same possibilities of outside control (objective verification on scales).

The present study of logical operations (i.e., operations which no longer tend to construct the object itself, but which tend, instead, to establish relations *between* objects) has shown, as originally hypothesized, that blind children continue to encounter difficulties—when such operations are based on material which can be handled and which characteristically is structured on the perceptual plane.

In the first section of Chapter 5, which compared the performances of blind and sighted children in perceptual tasks of classification and seriation there was discussion of the superiority of the adventitiously blind over the congenitally blind. These results confirm those obtained by McAndrew (1948) and particularly those by Axelrod (1959). McAndrew ascribes such difficulties to the greater mental rigidity of the blind which is due to their social isolation. By contrast, Axelrod interprets his results within a Hebbian framework: early visual deprivation is followed by a general conceptual deficiency because the deprivation diminished the child's interaction with his environment and reduced the possibilities of early training.

Present experimentation has shown that the handicap of blindness does not exert a homogenous influence on the different sectors of intellectual activity. While partially confirming Axelrod's interpretation, the results also introduce operation nuances.

Review of findings reveal that performance of the blind approximates that of the sighted most closely in the area of verbal-logical operations. What is the significance of such an observation?

In Chapter 1 it was indicated that although blindness caused perceptual deficits it did not prevent normal development of language; in fact, a tendency toward verbal hypertrophy was noted.

In verbal reasoning, the blind and the sighted theoretically occupy analogous situations, both have only to handle the collective signs, learned and automatized the same way.

While it is true that language permits the conveyance of concepts and non-perceptual relations, one important category of words (the "object-words") are nothing but the symbolic and conventional expression of material reality (an orange, a horse, a fish, etc.), and this material reality is apprehended differently by the blind and by the sighted. Thus, for these two groups, the same verbal signs do not have identical meaning because they do not refer to equivalent perceptions.

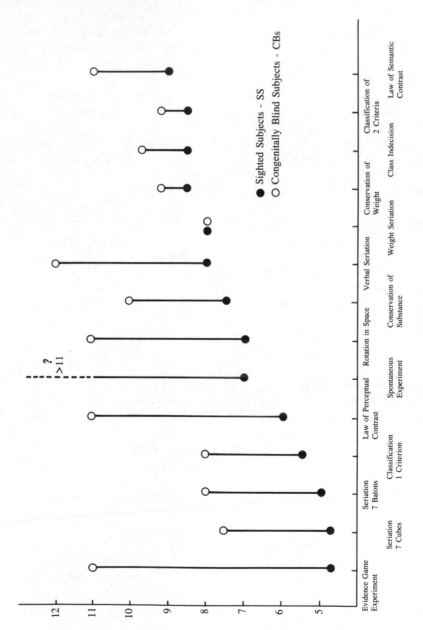

Fig. 26 Classification of tasks according to the function of the mean age by which they are achieved by sighted subjects.

It has been established that concrete reasoning precedes verbal reasoning in the sighted; present results supply confirmation. One then would surmise that the same sequence of development would exist for the blind, and that, as a consequence, their delay in perceptual logical operations would automatically be followed by a delay in verbal-logical operations; but present results show that this is not the case.

Differences in verbal-logical operations between the congenitally blind and the sighted are minimal or non-existent. Admittedly, this finding raises a problem: what are the true relations between the concrete and the verbal sectors? and how is the transition from one to the other achieved during the development of the individual? Or, to use Pavlovian terminology, how can the "second signal system" develop normally if the "first system" is characterized by insufficiencies?

Review of Figure 25 indicates that time span between acquisitions is not as great for the blind as for the sighted. Figure 26 is similar to Figure 25, but the order of the tasks has been sequentially arranged in terms of the mean age for successes of sighted subjects. Differences in the distribution of ages of success between blind and sighted children is striking.

For the blind ther eis a quasi-simultaneous appearance of the two forms of reasoning, and the concrete presentation of objects upon which the operations are based does not accelerate the resolution of these problems.

This emphasizes the fundamental differences in the behavior of the sighted and of the blind when they are confronted with the same problems.

The simultaneous emergence of differing logical structures in the blind child is of particular significance: it suggests that verbal operations can develop in a relatively autonomous way even though a grave deficiency exists at the concrete level. This rather surprising phenomenon is not only in opposition to Piaget's position (i.e., the action by the subject on the object always constitutes the first step in the acquisition of knowledge), but also to related psychological and educational literature. The point will be explored in the following discussion of respective roles of figurative structures and language in the development of intellectual operations in the child.

Figurative Structures, Language and Function

To differentiate concrete and verbal operations, considerations will be given to the role of figurative structures and language first in concrete and then in verbal operations.

Figurative Structures and Language in Concrete Operations

Role of figurative structures

Blindness has been defined as a restriction of figurative knowledge. If this knowledge were really an "obstacle" to logical reasoning, the blind would achieve operatory thought earlier than the sighted. Actually, this was not observed in our experimental results. On the contrary, the inferior performance of the blind supplies a measure of the advantage taken by the sighted from the variety of perceptual inputs they receive. Therefore, restricting perceptual data does not constitute a help in solving the so-called "conflict" between perception and reasoning. Alternatively, in the sighted, the wide range of perceptual data available accelerates the coordination of the various apparent aspects of objects into an invariant and stable world.

This does not contradict Bruner's findings (1964a; 1964b) showing that in conservation tasks, conservation appears earlier if some critical cues are masked (i.e., the level of the poured water). Since blindness results in a general and not a specific perceptual restriction, it still allows the tactual perception of the conflicting cues (i.e., the length of the plasticine sausage).

On the other hand, difficulties encountered by the blind manifest themselves only through delayed acquisition, and not in the form of permanent inabilities. Moreover, the style of successes and failures in the blind and in the sighted is the same. This discards the notion that "the world of the blind" is basically different from the world of the sighted in either the spatial or the logical domain.

Therefore, present research confirm what psychology and education have already taught about the child's reasoning. Since Maria Montessori, "new" education has stressed in the young child the higher efficiency of didactic methods using concrete material. The same emphasis emerges from Piaget's theory: in equivalent areas of thought, "concrete" operational structures are formed prior to "formal" ones.

Nevertheless, when Piaget (1960) has opposed the "figurative" aspects of knowledge to the "operative" ones, he has somewhat devaluated the role of perception and of mental images in logical reasoning (according to him, figurative structures are subordinated to operative ones). Actually, the logical development of the blind shows that two aspects of knowledge are closely linked and that both strongly contribute to the improvement of rational thinking.

There is note, however, that nothing in our results allows the conclusion that figurative aspects are the true origins of operations and that they are sufficient to account for the development of intelligence. All that can be said is that difficulties in blind children confirm the "necessary" character of this form of learning as a condition preliminary to the consideration of certain concrete logical operations.

As to the superiority of the adventitiously blind over the congenitally blind in operations based on concrete manipulations, it confirms the importance attached by Piaget to the sensori-motor period (a point agreed to by many others, Hebb in particular). It is during this time that the main schemes of action are established and organized. Indeed, when blindness occurs later, the handicap has little influence on the organization of figurative structures and on the development of operatory ones.

Role of language
Results show that language, although normally developed in the blind, cannot compensate (at least at the initial stages of development) for the difficulties arising from limited and unorganized tactile-kinesthetic perceptions. For example, blind children

were all able to label verbally objects dimensions: "square," "round," "big," "small," etc.; nevertheless, they failed in the classification test using shape or size criteria.

Comparison between blind and deaf children may be of interest here. The difficulties of deaf children in abstract tasks have often been attributed to the language deficiency of these children, which would maintain them at a "perceptual level," But blindness, which restricts perception while perserving language abilities, has finally, similar effects on concrete tasks. This shows that logical development stems neither from language alone, nor from figurative structures alone: it rather stems from a close coordination and interaction of these two major cognitive tools.

The above remarks apply only to operations deriving from concrete manipulable objects. Consideration now is given to operations with a verbal base.

Figurative Structures and Language in Verbal Operations

Role of figurative structures
The development of verbal logical operations in the blind approximates development in the normal, although his perceptual structures and imagery are markedly inferior to those of the sighted of equivalent ages. In other words, alteration of figurative learning does not seem to have any specific effect on the development of verbal logic. The relative autonomy of the verbal sector seems in contradiction to the close interdependence found between figurative structures and language during the development of concrete operations. While results obtained by Oleron (1952) and others have shown that deprivation of language in the deaf is followed by deficits in certain concrete logical activities, it appears, conversely, that visual deprivation which considerably reduces the possibilities of the blind's perceptive apprehension has only very few repercussions on his construction of verbal operations.

If we do not find a rigorous parallelism between the role of language in concrete operations and the role of figurative aspects in verbal operations, perhaps it is because the situations created by blindness and deafness are not, themselves, parallel. Although the congenitally blind lacks multiplicity and richness of visual input, he still has the use of an instrument of perceptual learning, tactual apprehension which, despite its limitations, does provide information about the world of objects. For this reason reference has been made to a "reduction," impoverishment," or "alteration" of the figurative structures of the congenitally blind as compared to those of the sighted, but never to total deprivation: this would be absurd.

On the contrary, the congenitally deaf is in a much more critical situation. His deprivation of language, being quasi-complete, also influences the non-verbal aspects of "abstract" operations which bear on concrete objects. The effect on verbal operations certainly would have been different if a subject also were totally deprived of tactile-kinesthetic representations; fortunately, such deprivation does not occur, even in pathology.

Role of language

The remarks which follow are derived from responses made by the blind to simple tasks of verbal reasoning. The development of verbal logical reasoning has been found to be relatively normal in the congenitally blind. Thus, language allows a certain form of operativity to occur. By assigning conventional and easily accessible signs to objects, language liberates the blind from his difficulties to cope with material reality demands having a level of complexity superior to his logical and perceptive capabilities. Although the verbal signs he uses lack in precision, richness and, at times, in meaning, verbal reasoning does permit exercise of intellectual potentials. For instance, some blind children, as old as nine or ten years, may maintain that a fish has four legs or a wing or a beak; but at the same time, they classify the fish as an "animal" or "a thing that eats" or a "living thing," etc.

In the language of the blind, a word often has a vague reference stripped of its particular attributes (cf. notion of "verbalism"). But if the blind student is provided indications of the hierarchical ordering of classes ("daisies are flowers," "fishes are animals," etc.), and on relations ("Peter is taller than Paul," etc.) language allows the normal exercise of verbal logic, an activity in which the blind child can engage. On the contrary, when this logical activity involves actual objects, it is disturbed by the multiple aspects under which objects are perceived, and the blind child generally is unable to integrate these various aspects into a mobile and coherent system.

Relation Between the Development of Concrete and Verbal Operations

Disabilities observed in the blind, and disabilities observed in aphasia and dyspraxia indicate that the three involve operations which are not systematically interdependent: i.e., one area can develop quasi-normally in spite of a disorder in the other.

This fact is not new. What is new is the observed *inversion in the order of acquisition*. Previously, the observed order was one which proceeded from the "concrete" level to one more "abstract" and more verbal. However, the operative development of the blind indicates that this order is not obligatory. In some cases when a blind person finds it difficult or impossible to engage in concrete reasoning, language may bridge the way from an incoherent material reality to rational thought. For this reason blindness is considered less handicapping than deafness.

Under these conditions, it may be hypothesized that in the blind child the development of concrete processes will be accelerated when certain verbal logical structures have been formed. The late successes of the blind on concrete tasks probably depend on much more elaborate mechanisns than the early successes of the sighted. It is not just feedback from the operative structures to figurative ones. The development of the former allows for a better organization of the latter. In the establishment of operatory systems, progress in the verbal sector probably promotes the evolution of the concrete sector.

To verify this hypothesis, it would be necessary to follow, over time, the development of blind children and determine if lags observed at the concrete level were totally overcome during adolescence. Such verification is beyond the scope of the present study.

Is the role played by language in the development of reasoning in the blind congruent with Piaget's theory of cognitive development? According to him, language is "perhaps necessary" for progression to the formal level, but it is only a symbolic system which cannot be fully utilized until the logical structures which are prerequisite to its handling are formed. These logical structures have their origin neither in perception nor in language, but in the progressive coordination of the sensory-motor schemes of action on the objects. At first the action involves real objects; later it involves representative and symbolic ones. The blind exhibit insufficiencies in coordination of schemes involving concrete objects; however, this insufficiency does not delay the coordination of actions involving symbolic objects, words, and verbal signs.

This means that in some exceptional situations, the verbal system may manifest some coordinations and generalizations not deriving directly from perceptual-motor activity with objects. Thus, the sighted child seems to develop his logical potentialities mainly through activity on real objects when he is young, while the blind have to develop these logical potentialities mainly through the world of conventional signs.

Visual Deprivation and Learning: Relations Between Object and Subject

Within the framework of Piaget's theory, and on both biological and intellectual planes, the concepts of *assimilation* and *accommodation* govern the equilibrium between the organism and its environment. Accommodation is defined by Piaget as the pressures exercised by objects on the individual (object acting on the subject), while assimilation is the process through which outside data are inserted in the scheme of behavior (subject acting on objects). This double mechanism of assimilation of data to existing structures of thought, and of accommodation of thought to the always new demands of reality, is the base of the individual's intelligent activity.

In Piaget's approach, figurative structures tend toward maximum accommodation because perceptions and representative imagery, emerging from imitative mechanisms, are oriented toward the copy of the object and the individual's adjustment to this object. On the contrary, it is the dynamic equilibrium between assimilation and accommodation which characterizes operativity.

Under these conditions, blindness, which was originally defined as an alteration of the figurative act of knowing, can also be defined as an alteration of the capabilities of accommodation to the outside reality. However, as demonstrated in the present study, the alteration of capacities for accommodation are not followed by a corresponding deficiency in the possibility of assimilation.

In other words, early blindness introduces a *rupture of equilibrium* between these two processes; the blind child has the use of all the intellectual instruments necessary for the integration of outside data, but is deprived of a great part of the means by which the sighted child controls his adjustments to reality. Because less pressure is exercised by the outside world (i.e. unlike the sighted child he does not have opportunity to verify the adequacy of his representations in relation to objective reality), the blind child assimilates perceived data through generalizations which long remain maladaptive and deforming. The difficulties he encounters in the logical structuring of the real world are manifestations of the disequilibrium existing between untouched assimilatory potentialities and a deeply deficient accommodative system of control. Thus there is a clarification of the role played by figurative structures in the acquisition of knowledge. They transmit the multiple aspects of the object to the sighted individual, and in so doing, safeguard him from incorrect systematizations; they promote intellectual accommodation by presenting contradictions which provide comparison between the adequacy of his knowledge and reality.

The figurative alteration which characterizes blindness does not have such intense repercussions on verbal logical reasoning: on this plane, direct control is, perhaps, not as imperative as it is on the concrete plane. Because the symbolic signs continue to correspond to material reality the blind child can apply assimilatory activity to verbal reasoning even when these signs are stripped of a portion of their meaning.

Although the constitution of logical structures can be achieved by the blind, blindness seriously impairs the ability of accommodation on an "experimental" return to reality. Thus, frequently the blind child operates within a verbal system which is handled more easily than is the world of objects, but which, if its ties to reality are lost, becomes a closed and necessarily inadequate system.

The notion of "verbalism" (Cutsforth, 1951; Henri, 1948; Harley, 1964) is generally defined as the blind child's use of words for which he does not have an accurate understanding. It should be extended to include verbal constructions which have not met the test of reality.

Educational implications may be derived from the study: *there should be an effort to promote interaction between the child and his environment, and to emphasize the tactual perceptive exploration of objects in order to counterbalance, in part, the negative effects of a sensory deprivation which does not affect the intellectual operative ability of the child.*

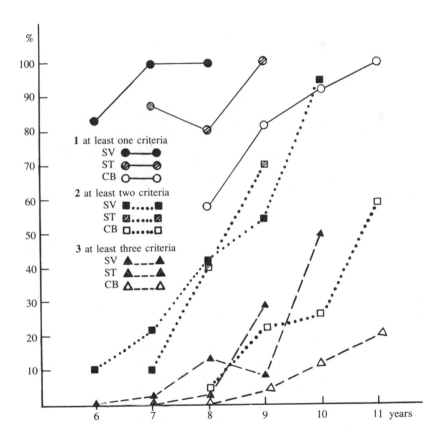

Fig. 15 Percentages of subjects one criterion, using two criteria, and using all three criteria of classification.

AFTERWORD

by Beth Stephens

Seventeen years elapsed between the initial publication of Yvette Hatwell's *Priva-tion sensorielle et intelligence* and the present English translation. Because of this time lag, English speaking professionals in the field of visual impairment, generally, have been aware of Hatwell's work, but have not had the opportunity to accord it the detailed review that is now possible. However, despite the language barrier, one finds frequent reference to Hatwell's application of Piagetian theory in subsequent reports of research on spatial concepts, mental images and cognitive development in blind children (e.g., Simpkins, 1979a, 1979b; Hall, 1981).

An additional major effort which used Hatwell's work as a guide, and which involved assessment, intervention and staff training was conducted by Stephens and Simpkins (1974); in this comparative study on the development of Piagetian reasoning in 75 sighted congenitally blind subjects (CA 6–18; IQ 90–110) it was found that, when compared to sighted subjects, the congenitally blind subjects exhibited average reasoning delays of four to eight years. A subsequent second project, which utilized a stratified sample of congenitally blind (13 treatment; 13 nontreatment) and sighted (13 nontreatment) subjects drawn from the group of subjects used in the first study, provided evidence that reasoning delays can be ameliorated through appropriate intervention experiences (Stephens, Grube, and Fitzgerald, 1977). The research efforts of the staff and consultants for these two earlier projects provided the framework for the third and final study. A Piagetian Approach to Visually Handicapped Education (Stephens and Grube, 1980), a nationwide project which was designed to train teachers of the visually impaired in the utilization of Piagetian reasoning assessments and in the design, implemen-tation and evaluation of reasoning activities. These projects provide support for Hatwell's earlier findings on the cognitive delays experienced by blind persons; they also serve to demonstrate that if individually appropriate intervention ac-tivities are provided by teachers who are aware of the need for blind students to interact purposefully with objects and people in their environment, significant cognitive development generally will result.

Thus, there has been continuing effort to extend knowledge of thought proc-esses in blind persons. In the years between the French and English publications of Hatwell's research on cognitive development in blind persons, she, too, has continued the analysis of perception and cognition. Her recent discussion of form perception and related issues in blind humans (Hatwell, 1978) provides a critical view of research concerning the general characteristics of haptic form perception in the blind. In her discussion on the nature of intersensory relations in childhood, Hatwell notes that both Gibson (1969) and Bower (1974) posit that, although *there is initially an undifferentiated state,* with time the infant experiences progressive differentiation between modalities (e.g., vision and haptic). Conversely, Piaget (1935) holds there "is a progressive coordination between sensory spheres that are at first dissociated (Hatwell, 1978, p. 512)." However, as Hatwell notes, Gibson and Piaget agree that both haptic and visual processes are subjected to the same laws and have a common mode of functioning, and that each modality that participates in the polysensorial system will improve when there is progress in another modality or in the entire system; i.e., haptic perception benefits from perceptual learning which accrues from the visual modality, and there is improvement in early development when visual and haptic perception become combined. Hatwell asks if the adventitiously blind person has an advantage over the congenitally blind person, because during infancy the person who is not yet blind can establish and coordinate basic schemes that later will be useful when he/she has to formulate, on a haptic basis, concepts of the physical world. Her conclusion is that definitive statements on differences between congenitally and adventitiously blind persons cannot be made because, except for Fraiberg's (1968) work, no pertinent experimental work on the perceptual and cognitive development of blind babies is available.

As attempt is made to answer the question, "Do visual haptic modalities convey equivalent information?" Hatwell (1978) reviews research in terms of Revesz' (1950) position "(autonomy and possibility of specific laws in each modality) and Gibson's (1966) position (equivalence of the processes and of the information carried by each modality, p. 154)," and concludes no fundamental facts have evolved which support the position that specific laws govern each modality, visual and haptics. Isolated data, particularly that involving the tactile-vision-substitution system (Bach and Rita, 1972; White et al., 1970) tend to support Gibson's position of "modality equivalence and central processing of higher-order variables." However, Hatwell (1978) suggests:

> To really know if the spatial constructs formed by vision and haptics are of the same nature, it would be useful to systematically compare CB [congenitally blind] and NS [normally sighted] subjects in the perception of shape properties and of spatial transformations belonging to different geometries (and especially the topological one), not merely to Euclidian geometry. Only in these conditions would structual differences appear, if they actually exist (p. 517).

Thus, Hatwell has continued her inquiry into the thought processes of blind persons, and as she has done so she has not only suggested answers, but also has supplied questions that promise to provide continuing motivation to persons conducting research in this area.

GLOSSARY

by Beth Stevens

Accommodation: or outer adaptation, serves as a complement to assimiliation and occurs when environmental conditions require coping which necessitates a modification, revision or rearrangement of existing mental structures or schemas (Stephens, 1968, p. 31).

Amblyopia: "dimness of sight without apparent change in the eye structures, associated especially with toxic effects of dietary deficiencies, amblyopic—adjective" (Webster's New Collegiate Dictionary, 1974, p. 36).

Assimilation: the incorporation of data or material from the environment into existing internal thought structures (Stephens, 1968, p. 31).

Classification: the way we mentally structure or group information that comes to us through our senses; we organize things mentally by creating classes, breaking large classes into sub-classes and by reclassifying on a different criterion. During the concrete stage of cognitive development a person becomes capable of adding classes together, multiplying classes, and dividing classes into smaller units.

Concrete Operation: mental activities which characterize Piaget's third (concrete) stage of cognitive development, these operations involve logical reasoning at a concrete rather than abstract level. Objects or events are classified, compared for similarities or differences, located in space or time, evaluated or counted. These cognitive classifications, seriations, or systems of explanation are termed "groupings" and they last thoughout a person's life. The integrated, intellectual system achieved through grouping is used in organizing and manipulating the surrounding world. The thought structure makes possible such intellectual operations as addition, subtraction, multiplication, division, comparing classes and relations of objects and events, measurement of time and space, as well as operations which involve systems of values and interpersonal interaction. The distinguishing characteristic of the mobile equilibration which promotes groupings is that thought is no longer centered on a particular state of an object, but can follow successive changes through various types of detours and reversals. Because the operations involved at this stage are constantly tied to action, they are concrete, not formal, operations. Children at this stage may be incapable of these processes if there is no manipulation of concrete objects, i.e., if reasoning involves only verbal propositions (Stephens, 1963, p. 79).

Conservation: realization that structure or quantity (amount, weight, volume) is invariant although physical change may occur; e.g, two identical balls of clay will continue to contain the same amount even though one ball is transformed into the shape of a hot dog; i.d., there is "conservation of substance."

Conservation of Volume: realization that the volume of an article remains constant despite change in its shape; example, if a ball of clay is immersed in a glass of water, the water level will rise; later if the ball of clay is broken into 20 small pieces and the pieces are immersed in the glass of water, the water will rise to the same level as it did when the ball was immersed; the volume of the object is conserved despite changes in form.

Conservation of Weight: realization that the weight of an object does not change even if there is change in shape; example: stretching a rubber band until it is twice its previous length does not alter its weight; the weight is "conserved."

Decalage: "time lag or temporal displacement, is a downward dropping movement from one plane to another and is used to refer to aspects of cognitive development that appear at a stage subsequent to the one at which they are normally expected" (Stephens, 1968, p. 31).

Decentration: simultaneous consideration of several aspects of a situation. For example, a young child is presented with two clay balls, equal in amount; then, as he observes, one of the balls is rolled into a hot dog. A young child will note that the hot dog is longer and conclude it has more clay. He neglects to note that although the hot dog is longer than the clay ball it is not as wide. He is not *decentering*, simultaneously taking both length and width into account; instead his thought centers on the length of the object to the exclusion of the width.

Deferred Imitation: the ability to imitate an action after the action is over. To engage in deferred imitation one must maintain a mental image of the action.

Displacement: "a change of place with reference to a preliminary placing. . . . Let there be a series of elements arranged in sequence ABCD. . . according to a linear order. . . . Thus posited, one element will be said to be displaced if it changes its sequence and follows those terms which is formerly preceded: e.g., A will be displaced in relation to B and C, if it comes to occupy the place situated behind C and if ABCD. . . is therefore transformed into BCAD. . . so that A which preceded B and C comes after them at the end of its displacement" (Gruber and Voneche, 1977, p. 539–540).

Equilibration: Piaget posits the mechanism that accounts for the transition from one stage of cognitive development to the next four factors, heredity and maturation, social interaction and, physical experiences, equilibration; equilibration coordinates development in the other three areas (Rosen, 1977, p. 28). Piaget believes intellectual development has its own pace and rhythm and involves the same kind of organismic regulation as do physiological and motivational processes. He conceives of equilibration as a mechanism of change and continuity, a state of balance between competing actions; a system is in equilibration when a perturbation which modifies the state of the system has its counterpart in a spontaneous action which compensates for its effect (Gardner, 1974, p 104).

Empiricism: "the view that the infant is born with no innate ideas, and that all knowledge results from the accumulation of experience, so that knowledge is a direct copy of the reality with which each person is incessantly confronted" (Gruber and Voneche, 1977, p. xviii).

Esthesiometer: "an instrument for measuring sensory discrimination; especially one for determining the distance by which two points pressed against the skin must be separated in order that they may be felt as separate" (Webster's New Collegiate Dictionary, 1974, p. 391).

Figurative Knowing (Thought): "the forms of cognition which, from the subject's point of view, appear as "copies of reality". . . . Three varieties of figurative knowledge are perception, imitation and mental images" (Gruber and Voneche, 1977, p. 653).

Figurative Representations: refers to "those aspects of thought that are related more directly to the states of objects than to their transformations. . ." (Gruber and Voneche, 1977, p. 645).

Formal Operations: characterizes Piaget's fourth and final stage of cognitive development; there is ability to think abstractly, to formulate and use hypotheses, engage in propositional thinking and combinatorial logic; at this stage there is a type of thinking about thinking, logical deductions are possible. Thought is said to "operate on operations" rather than on concrete objects.

Glioma: a tumor composed of tissue which represents neuroglia in any one of its stages of development (Dorland's Illustrated Medical Dictionary, 1965, p. 618).

Groupings: "the first operational structures are called 'groupings' and give the child the means to know the world within stable systems of logical classifications, seriation, numbers, spatial and temporal coordinates, and causality. These systems permit reversible operations, acts of knowing that can move within the system in reverse directions, e.g., from part to whole or from before to after and vice versa" (Furth, 1969, p. 247).

Infralogical Operations: are operations which "apply no longer to the nesting of parts of the same object into the total object, replacing the notion of resemblance by that of proximity, the notion of difference in general by that of difference in order of placement... and the notion of number by that of measure" (Battro, p. 94). Infralogical operations are operations which involve a representative imagery and which promote consideration of such spatial relationships as space and time, proximity and separation.

Interactionist: one who subscribes to the theory that cognitive development proceeds as a person interacts with his enviroment, the persons and things around him; the importance of the person and of the environment is recognized but its is the *interaction* that is emphasized.

Interiorization: "leads from 'practical' to operational intelligence and is the precondition for objective knowledge as well as for symbolic representation" (Furth, 1969, p. 262).

Intuitive: the second stage of preoperational thought, "a gradual coordination of relations leads the child from a preconceptual or symbolic acquisition stage to one in which these symbols or words may be manipulated in operational thought. Although processes are often rapid, the intelligence remains prelogical. Reasoning is intuitive. Even though the child observes two small glasses, A and B, identical in size and shape and each is filled with an equal number of beads, and in turn observes as the beads from glass A are emptied into another glass A^1 which is taller and narrower, he tends to conclude that the quantity of beads has changed. A^1 contains more than B because "it is higher". . . . Error is perceptual in nature. Thinking is influenced by what is seen at that given moment" (Stephens, 1966, p. 78–79).

Invariance of Thought: realization that despite changes in state or form of an object its amount is maintained or conserved.

Logico–Mathematical: Piaget states that logic "is the basis of all elementary thought structures, and particularly those which antedate mathematization (Piaget 1949b, p. 99). In this sense Piaget uses the term logico-mathemactial to refer to all those structures characterized either by mathematical principles or by more primitive or elementary principles of logic (Chandler, 1969, p. 11; Stephens, 1968, p. 33). Logico-mathematical operations are those which establish relations between given objects, e.g. classification, seriation, numbers, similarities and differences.

Logic of Propositions: involves evaluation of the validity of a line of reasoning apart from its factual content; the logical link between premises and conclusions is established independent of the content of that particular proposition (Gruber and Voneche, 1977, p. 395).

Mental Image: a mental likeness of a perceived or perceptible phenomenon that can be represented in visual, auditory, tactile or other sensory forms. Since images are mental constructs, the extent to which they resemble the concrete phenomena they represent varies. Mental images serve as a means of representing the environment and of formulating thoughts in addition to language (Hall, 1981, p. 281).

Muller–Lyer Illusion: "the distorted perception of length when a line has arrow heads, or reverse arrow heads or 'feathers' in the figure, $\longleftrightarrow$ or $\succ\!\!\!-\!\!\!\prec$; the former looks shorter, the latter longer, than an unadorned straight line" (English and English, 1958 p. 332).

Nystagmus: "a rapid involuntary oscillation of the eyeball" (Webster's New Collegiate Dictionary, 1974, p. 790).

Object Permanence: the realization that an object continues to exist although it is no longer seen or perceived through the senses.

Operation (mental): an interiorized and reversible (mental) action (Stephens, 1968, p. 33). Piaget holds that the origin of operations is the activity of the subject rather than merely in his perceptions.

Operational Thought: refers to Piaget's two final stages of cognitive development, concrete reasoning, which is logical but concrete, and formal reasoning, which can be abstract rather than concrete.

Operative Knowing: an act of transformation through which incoming data are understood. . . the object as it exists outside the knower does not provide the *meaning* to him, for this is derived as an assimilation to the operative structure of the image" (Rosen, 1977, p. 88, 89).

Operativity: "is the essential, generalizable structuring aspects of intelligence insofar as knowing means constructing, transforming, incorporating, etc." (Furth, 1969, p. 263).

Preconceptual: the first substage of Piaget's second or preoperational stage of cognitive development; during this period concepts are being formed. Preconcepts are the meaning the child attaches to his early verbal symbols and tend to be midway between general and individual meaning.

Prelogical Thought: in Piagetian terms is thought which has not achieved the level of logical reasoning which characterizes the third or concrete stage of cognitive development. Levy–Bruhl uses the term "prelogical thought" as thought whose only logic is that of emotions, or thought which can contain a fusion of fact and magic (Gruber and Voneche, 1977, p. 56).

Quantification: "Piaget, after Kant, distinguishes two sorts of quantities: Intensive quantification deals only with the relation between the part and the whole. It is clear without counting, that a part of something numerable is smaller than the whole. Or in more general terms, that a subclass of a set contains fewer elements than the class itself. . . . Extensive quantification appears when the differences themselves are compared. A special case of extensivequantification is metric quantification in which all differences are compared to a standard measure of which they are either a multiple or a fraction" (Gruber and Voneche, 1977, p. 344).

Rationalism: "a theory that reason is in itself a source of knowledge superior to and independent of sense perceptions; a view that reason and experience rather than the nonrational are the fundamental criteria in the solution of problems" (Webster's New Collegiate Dictionary, 1974, p. 958).

Representational Level: ability to think about or deal with something not present; thought at the representational level is no longer tied to external acts (Furth, 1969).

Reversibility: is the capacity of inversing an operation of mind or the ability to study a problem from two opposite viewpoints. "We will define reversibility as the capacity to execute a particular action or annul it while remaining cognizant that it constitutes the same action (Piaget, Apostel, and Mandelbrot, 1957, p. 44) An example of "reversibility of thought" is found in the successful performance of the reasoning assessment "Conservation of Substance." In this assessment two balls of clay, identical in amount and shape, are displayed, then as the subject watches, one ball is rolled into a hot dog. Following this the subject is asked if there is the same amount of clay in the presently observed ball and hot dog. To correctly answer "there is" the subjects reverses his thought processes and thinks back to the point in time when the two were equivalent clay balls. After engaging in this "reversibility" he reasons they are still the same, only the shape is changed (Stephens, 1968, p. 33).

Schema: that aspect of an operation that is generalizable and assimilable (Gruber and Voneche, 1977, p. 512).

Scheme: is the part of an action that is transferable to the same situations or is generalizable in an analogous situation. In genetic psychology a scheme is an active mental structure which deforms and reforms by assimilating the environment or accommodating to it. "The scheme of an action is, by definition, the structural ensemble of the generalizable characteristics of that action, that is to say, those which permit the repetition of the same action or its application to new concepts. The scheme of an action is, however, neither perceptible (one may perceive a particular action but not its scheme) nor directly available to introspection. One becomes aware of its implications only through repeating the action and comparing its successive results (Piaget and Beth, 1961, p. 251; Stephens, 1968, p. 34).

Sensory–Motor: "The characteristic mode of knowledge of Piaget's first stage of intelligence in which the form of knowledge is tied to the content of specific sensory input or motoric actions. Also referred to as practical intelligence" (Furth, 1969, p. 264).

Seriation: arranging objects in a series or succession, e.g., from longest to shortest. A Piagetian task termed "Seriation of Sticks" requires the ordering from longest to shortest of ten wooden dowels (which are one-half inch in diameter but which vary from one to ten inches).

Signifiers: In Piaget's theory of symbolization "meaning is understood as the relationship between a *signified,* which is an object or action, and a *signifier*, which stands for it. He distinguishes three sorts of *signifiers:* the *index,* which is an integral part of the signified, the *sign,* which is arbitrarily linked with the signified, and the *symbol,* which exhibits some analogical correspondence with the signified. For instance the ringing of the telephone is an *index,* a word is a *sign,* and using a stick as a gun is a *symbol.* In addition, *signs* are always *social signifiers,* whereas *symbols* can be *social* or individual signifiers. The symbolism of dreams is individual; in contrast the symbolism of games is social" (Gruber and Voneche, 1977, p. 485).

Signification: the relation of symbol (e.g. word, picture) to its thinking user. "Insignification is found a symbol's direct reference or meaning" (Furth, 1966, p. 42).

Strabismus: "inability of one eye to attain binocular vision with the other because of inbalance of the muscles of the eyeball" (Webster's New Collegiate Dictionary, 1974, p. 1148).

Structure: "the general form, the interrelatedness of parts within an organized totality. Structure can often be used interchangeably with organization, system, form, coordination" (Furth, 1969, p. 265).

Structured Whole: refers to the movement of thought toward the construction of a whole; relationship between its parts are separable as well as integrated. "We speak of a structure... when elements are joined into a totality possessing certain wholistic properties and when the properties of the elements depend entirely or partially on the characteristics of the totality" (Piaget, Apostel, and Mandelbrot, 1957, p. 34; Stephens, 1968, p. 34).

Symbolic Representations: the use of language, symbolic play, deferred imitation, etc., to internalize actions into thoughts.

Transitivity: "the ability to draw conclusions about two elements through comparison with an intermediary element. For example, if A equals B and B equals C, then it follow that A equals C" (Rosen, 1977, p. 19).

Verbalism: the use of words not verified by concrete experience (Cutsforth T.D., 1951).

BIBLIOGRAPHY

Ajuriaguerra, J. de, & Hegaen, C. H. *Le cortex cerebral.* Paris: Masson, 1960.

Ajuriaguerra, J. de, Guignard, F., Jaeggi, A., Kocher, F., Macquard, F., Pauniez, A., Quinopoz, D., & Siotis, E. Organisation psychologique et troubles de developpement du langage. Etude d'un groupe d'enfants dysphasiques. *Problemes de psycho-linguistique.* Paris: Presses Universitaires de France, 1963.

Axelrod, S. *Effects of early blindness. Performance of blind and sighted children on tactile and auditory tasks.* New York: American Foundation for the Blind, 1959.

Bach, Y., Rita, P. *Brain Mechanisms in sensory substitution.* New York: Academic Press, 1972.

Battro, A.M. *Piaget: Dictionary of Terms.* New York: Pergamon Press, 1973.

Bangerter, A. *Traitement de l'amblyopie.* Charleroi: Heraly, 1953.

Baumann, M. Studies in the application of motor skills techniques to the vocational adjustment of the blind. *Journal of Applied Psychology,* 1946, **30**, 144–154.

Baumann, M. *A manual of norms for tests used in counseling blind persons.* New York: American Foundation for the Blind, 1958.

Bean, C. H. The blind have "optical illusion." *Journal of Exp. Psychology,* 1938, **22**, 283–289.

Berkeley, G. Essai d'une theorie nouvelle de la vision. *Oeuvres choisies,* **I**. Paris: Aubier, 1944.

Beston, W. H., Heron, W., & Scott, T. H. Effects of decreased variation in the sensory environment. *Canadian Journal of Psychology,* 1954, **8**, 70–76.

Bingham, W. E., & Griffiths, W. J. The effect of different environments during infancy on adult behavior in the rat. *Journal of Comp. Physiol. Psychol.,* 1952, **45**, 307–312.

Bloom, B. S. *Stability and change in human characteristics.* New York: Wiley, 1964.

Blumenfeld, W. The relationship between the optical and haptic perception of space. *Acta Psychol.,* 1973, **2**, 125–175.

Borelli, M. La genese des operations logiques chez le sourd-muet. *Enfance,* 1951, **4**, 222–238.

Bouzas, A. Les resultats postoperatoires de la cataracte congenitale. *Arch. ophthal.,* 1955, **15**, 164–173.

Bower, T. G. R. *Development in infancy.* San Francisco: Freeman and Co., 1974.

Brattgard, S. O. The importance of adequate stimulation for the chemical composition of retinal ganglion cells during early post–natal development. *Acta Radiolog,* 1952, **96**, 1–80.

Bramaud du Boucheron, G. Current French research in developmental psychology. *International Journal of Behavioral Development,* 1983, **6**, 263–289.

Brekke, B., Williams, J. D., & Tait, P. The acquisition of conservation of weight by visually impaired children. *Journal of Genetic Psychology,* 1974, **125**, 89–97.

Brown, M. S., & Stratton, G. M. The spatial threshold of touch in blind and seeing children. *Journal of Exp. Psychol.,* 1925, **8**, 434–442.

Bruner, J. The cognitive consequence of early sensory deprivation. In Solomon, P. *Sensory Deprivation.* Cambridge: Harvard University Press, 1961.

Bruner, J. *Developpement de la perception et de l'intelligence chez l'enfant.* Conference prononcee a la Sorbonne en janvier, 1964a.

Bruner, J. The course of cognitive growth. *American Psychologist,* 1964b, **19**, 1–15.

Buell, C. E. Motor performance of visually handicapped children. Doctoral thesis, University of California, *Outlook for the Blind,* 1950, **44**, 256–258. *Journal of Exceptional Children,* 1950, **17**, 69–72.

Bullinger, A., & Chatillon, J. Recent theory and research of the Genevan school.

Flavell, J. H., & Markman, E. (Eds.), *Handbook of child psychology,* **III**: *Cognitive development.* New York: Wiley and Sons, 1983.

Burt, C. The development of reasoning in school children. *Journal of Exp. Pedag.,* 1919, **5**, 68–77 and 121–127.

Carr, H. A. The influence of visual guidance on maze-learning. *Journal of Exp. Psychol.,* 1921, **4**, 399–417.

Centre Epistemologie de Geneve. *Etudes d'Epistemologie Genetique,* **XVIII**.

Cheselden, W. An account of some observations made by a young gentleman, who was born blind, or lost his sight so early, that he had no rememberance of ever having seen, and was couch'd between 13 and 14 years of age. *Philosophical transactions of the Royal Society of London,* 1728, **35**, 447–540.

Chow, K. L., Riesen, A. H., & Newell, F. W. Degeneration of retinal ganglion cells in infant chimpanzees reared in darkness. *Journal Comp. Neurol.,* 1957, **107**, 27–42.

Critchley, M. Tactile thought with special reference to the blind. *Brain,* 1953, **76**, 19–35.

Cromer, R. F. Conservation by the congenitally blind. *British Journal of Psychology,* 1973, **64**, 241–250.

Cutsforth, T. D. *The blind in school and society.* New York: American Foundation for the Blind, 1951.

Delay, J. *Les astereognosies.* Paris: Masson, 1935.

Davidson, P. W., Dunn, G., Wiles-Kettenmann, M., & Appelle, S. Haptic conservation of amount in blind and sighted children: exploratory movements effects. *Journal of Pediatric Psychology,* 1981, **6**, 191–200.

Dennis, W. Congenital cataract and unlearned behavior. *Journal of Genet. Psychol.,* 1934, **44**, 340–351.

Diderot, D. *Lettres sur les aveugles a l'usage de ceux qui voient.* Paris: Garnier, 1956 (1st Ed. in 1749).

Diderot, D. *Lettre sur les sourds et muets a l'usage de ceux qui entendent et qui parlent.* Paris: Garnier, 1875.

Dorland's Illustrated Medical Dictionary. Philadelphia: W. B. Sanders, 1965.

Drever, J. Early learning and the perception of space. *American Journal of Psychology,* 1955, **68**, 604–614.

Duncan, D. K. A comparative study of finger-maze learning by blind and sighted subjects. *Journal genet. Psychol.,* 1934, **44**, 69–95.

English, H. B., & English, A. L. *A Comprehensive Dictionary of Psychological and Psychoanalytical Terms.* New York: Longmans, Green and Co., 1958.

Ewart, A. G., & Carp, F. M. Recognition of tactual form by sighted and blind subjects. *American Journal of Psychology,* 1963, **76**, 488–491.

Forgays, D. G., & Forgays, J. W. The nature of the effect of free environmental experience in the rat. *Journal comp. physiol. Psychol.,* 1952, **45**, 322–328.

Forgus, R. H. The effect of early perceptual learning on the behavioral organization of adult rats. *Journal comp. physiol. Psychol.,* 1954, **47**, 331–336.

Fraiberg, S. *Insights from the blind.* London: Souvenir Press, 1977.

Fraiberg, S. Parallel and divergent pattern in blind and sighted infants. *Psychoanalytical*

Study of the Child, **23**, 264–300.

Fraiberg, S., Barry, L., Siegel, M. D., & Gibson, R. The role of sound in the search behavior of a blind infant. *Psychoanalytical Study of the Child.*, 1966, **21**, 327–357.

Freedman, S. J., Grunebaum, H. U., & Greenblatt, M. Perceptual and cognitive changes in sensory deprivation. In Solomon P. et al., *Sensory Deprivation.* Cambridge: Harvard University Press, 1961.

Friedman, J., & Pasnak, R. Attainment of classification and seriation concepts by blind and sighted children. *Education of the visually handicapped,* 1973, **3–6**, 55–62.

Furth, H. G. *Piaget and Knowledge.* Englewood Cliffs, N.J.: Prentice-Hall, 1969.

Furth, H. G. *Thinking Without Language.* New York: The Free Press, 1966.

Galifret-Granjon, N. Les praxies chez l'enfant d'apres Piaget. *Psychiat. Enfant,* 1962, **4**(2), 579–591.

Gardner, H. *The Quest for Mind.* New York: Vintage Books, 1974.

Gelb, A., & Goldstein, K. Uber den Einfluss des vollstandigen Verlustes des optischen Vorstellungsvermogens auf das taktile Erkennen. *Z. Psychol. Physiol. der Sinnersorgane,* 1920, **83**, 1–94.

Gemelli, A. Sur quelques illusions dan le champ des sensations tactiles. *Arch. ital. Biol.,* 1913, **59**, 110–134.

Gibson, J. J. Observations on active touch, *Psychol. Rev.,* 1962, **69**, 477–491.

Gibson, J. J. *Principles of Perceptual Learning and Development.* New York: Appleton–Century Crofts.

Gibson, J. J. *The Senses considered as perceptual systems.* Boston: Houghton Mifflin, 1966.

Gottesman, M. Conservation development in blind children. *Child Development,* 1973, **44**, 824–827.

Greco, P. Apprentissage et structures intellectuelles. In Fraisse, P., & Piaget, J. M, *Traite de psychologie experimentale,* **VII**. Paris: Presses Universitaires de France, 1963, chap. 25.

Griesbach, H., Vergleichende Untersuchengen uber die Sinnescharfe Blinder und Sehender. *Arch. ges. Physiol.,* 1899, **74**, 577–638.

Grossiord, A. La reeducation des poliomyletiques et ses exigences. *Enfance,* 1961, 279–302.

Gruber, H. E., & Voneche, J. J. *The Essential Piaget.* New York: Basic Books, 1977.

Guillaumat, L., & Girard, G. Resultats fonctionnels des operations de cataracte congenitale. *Bull. Mem. Soc. Franc. Ophthalm.,* 1954, **67**, 343–356.

Hagen, F. W. Psychologie und Psychiatrie. In Rud. Wagners, *Handworterbuch der Physiologiq.,* **II**, 1844.

Haines, T. H. *Mental measurements of the blind: a provisional point scale and data for a year scale.* Princeton: Psychological Review, 1916.

Hall, A. Mental images and the cognitive development of the congenitally blind. *Journal of Visual Impairment & Blindness,* 1981, **75**, 281–285.

Harley, R. K. Jr. *Verbalism among blind children.* New York: American Foundation for the Blind, 1963.

Hatwell, Y. Perception tactile des formes et organisation spatiale tactile. *J. Psychol.,* 1959, **56**, 187–204.

Hatwell, Y. Etude de quelques illusions geometriques tactiles chez les aveugles. *Annee Psychol.,* 1960a, **60**, 11–27.

Hatwell, Y. La perception tactile des formes: perception et activite perceptive tactile. *J. Psychol.,* 1960b, **57**, 165–176.

Hatwell, Y. Role des elements figuratifs dans la genese des operations spatiales. *Etudes d'Epistemologie genetique,* **XVIII**: *L'epistemologie de l'espace.* Paris: Presses Universitaires de France, 1964, 173–201.

Hatwell, Y. Privation Sensorielle et Intelligence. Paris: Presses Universitaires de France, 1966.

Hatwell, Y. Form perception and related issues in blind humans. In Held, R., Leibowitz, H. W., & Teuber, H. L. (Eds.), *Handbook of sensory physiology,* **VIII**: *Perception.* New York and Berlin: Springer Verlag, 1978.

Hayes, S. P. New experimental data on the old problem of sensory compensation. *Teacher's Forum,* 1933, **6**, 22–26.

Hayes, S. P. Sensory compensation and the vicariate of the senses. *Outlook for the Blind,* 1934, **28**, 7–12, **36**, 67–71, 122–129.

Hayes, S. P. *Contribution to a psychology of blindness.* New York: American Foundation for the Blind, 1941.

Hayes, S. P. A second test scale for the mental measurement of the visually handicapped. *Outlook for the Blind,* 1943, **37**, 37–41.

Hayes, S. P. *Vocational aptitude tests for the blind.* Watertown: Perkins Institution, 1946.

Hebb, D. O. The innate organization of visual activity: I. Perception of figures by rats reared in total darkness. *J. Genet. Psychol.,* 1937, **51**, 101–126.

Hebb, D. O. The effects of early experience on problem-solving at maturity. *Amer. Psychologist,* 1947, **2**, 306–307.

Hebb, D. O. *The organization of behavior.* New York: Wiley, 1949.

Hebb, D. O. Discussion of sensory deprivation: Facts in search of a theory. *J. Nerv. Ment. Dis.,* 1961, **132**, 40–43.

Heidbredder, E. The attainment of concepts: VI. Exploratory experiments of conceptualization at perceptual levels. *J. Psychol.,* 1948, **26**, 193–216.

Heller, T. *Studien zur Blinden psychologie* (2nd Ed.). Leipzig: Wilhelm Engelmann, 1904.

Henri, P. Cecite et verbalisme. *J. Psychol. Norm. Path.,* 1948, **41**, 216–240.

Henri, P. *Les aveugles et la societe.* Paris: Presses Universitaires de France, 1958.

Heron, W. B., Bexton, W., & Hebb, D. O. Cognitive effect of decreased variation in the sensory environment. *Amer. Psychologist,* 1953, **8**, 366.

Higgins, L. C. *Classification in congenitally blind children.* New York: American Foundation for the Blind (Research Series), 1973.

Hunter, W. F. An analysis of space perception in congenitally blind and sighted individuals. *J. Gen. Psychol.,* 1964, **70**, 325–329.

Hunter, I. M. L. The solving of three-term series problems. *Brit. J. Psychol.,* 1957a, **48**, 286–298.

Hunter, I. M. L. A note on an atmosphere effect in adult reasoning. *Quart. J. Exp. Psychol.,* 1957b, **9**, 175–176.

Huteau, M. Dependance-independance a l'egard du champ et developpement de la pensee operatoire. *Archives de Psychologie,* 1980, **48**, 1–40.

Hymovitch, B. The effects of experimental variations on problem solving in the rat. *J. Comp. Psysiol. Psycol.,* 1952, **42**, 313–321.

Inhelder, B. *The diagnosis of reasoning in the mentally retarded.* New York: John Day, 1968 (first publication in French in 1943).

Inhelder, B., & Piaget, J. *De la logique de l'enfant a la logique de l'adolescent.* Paris: Presses Universitaires de France, 1955.

Inhelder, B. De la configuration perceptive a la structure operatoire. *Le probleme des* stades en psychologie de l'enfant. Paris: Presses Universitaires de France, 1956, 137-162.

Inhelder, B. *Communication prononcee au Congres europeen de Pedo-Psychiatrie*. Rome, 1963a.

Inhelder, B. Les operations de la pensee et leur symbolisme image, *Cahiers de Psychol*. (Ed. par la Societe de Psychologie du Sud-Est), 1963b, **3**, 143-171.

Inhelder, B., Ackermann-Valladeo, E., Blanchet, A., Karmiloff-Smith, A., Kilcher-Hagedorn, H., Montangero, J., & Robert, M. Des structures cognitives aux procedures de decouverte: esquisses de recherches en cours. *Archives de Psychologie*, 1976, **44**, 57-72.

Inhelder, B., & Piaget, J. Procedures et structures. *Archives de Psychologie*, 1979, **47**, 165-176.

Katz, D. *Der Aufbau der Tastwelt*. Leipzig: Johann Ambrosius Barth, 1925.

Knotts, J. R., & Miles, W. R. The maze-learning ability of blind compared with sighted children. *Journal genet. Psychol.*, 1929, **36**, 21-50.

Koch, H. L., & Ufkess, J. A. A comparative study of stylus maze learning by blind and subjects. *Journal exp. Psychol.*, 1926, **9**, 118-131.

Krause, A. C. Effects of retrolental fibroplasis in children. *Arch. Ophthal., Chicago*, 1955, **53**, 522-529.

Kunz, M. *The physiology of the blind*. Washington: Volta Bureau, 1908.

Lairy, G. C., Netchine, S., & Neyraut, M. T. L'enfant deficient visuel. *Psychiat. Enfant.*, 1962, **5**, 357-440.

Langan, I. W. *Instruction-booklet for a special adaptation for the blind of the 1937 Revision of the Stanford Binet Tests*. Bristol: Burden mental Res. Dept., 1945.

Lautrey, J. L'Equilibration suffit-elle a guider la coordination des actions? *Psychologie Francaise*, 1981, **26**, 259-281.

Leibnitz, G. W. *Nouveaux essais sur l'entendement humain*. Paris: Charpentier, 1842.

Lende, H. *Books about the blind, a bibliographical guide to literature relating to the blind*. New York: American Foundation for the Blind, 1953.

Levine, J., & Blackburn, A. R. Intelligence test scores of newly blinded soldiers. *Journal Consult. Psychol.*, 1950, **14**, 311-315.

Locke, J. *Essays concerning human understanding*. Oxford: Clarendon Press, 1936.

London, I. D. A Russian report on the post-operative newly seeing. *American Journal of Psychology*, 1960, **73**, 478-482.

Longeot, F. *Les stades operatoires et les facteurs de l'intelligence*. Grenoble: Presses Universitaires de Grenoble, 1978.

Lowenfeld, B. Psychological problems in children with impaired vision. In Cruickshank, W. M., *Psychology of exceptional children and youth*. Englewood Cliffs: Prentice-Hall, 1955.

Markman, E. M. Empirical versus logical solutions to part-whole comparison problems concerning classes and collections. *Child Development*, 1978, **49**, 168-171.

Maxfield, K., & Buchholz, S. *A social maturity scale for blind preschool children: a guide* to its use. New York: American Foundation for the Blind, 1957.

McAndrew, H. Rigidity and isolation: A study of the deaf and the blind. *Journal of Abnormal Soc. Psychol.*, 1948, **43**, 476-494.

McLaughlin, S. C. Visual perception in strabismus and amblyopia. *Psychol. Monogr.*, 1964, **78**, 12.

McFarland, D. C. An exploratory study comparing the maze learning ability of blind and sighted subjects. *New Outlook for the Blind,* 1952, **46,** 259–263.

Millar, S. Spatial representation by blind and sighted subjects. *Journal of Experimental Child Psychology,* 1976, **12,** 460–479.

Millar, S. Cross-modal and intersensory perception and the blind. In Walk, R., & Pick, H. L. *Intersensory perception and sensory integration.* New York: Plenum Press, 1981.

Miller, C. K. Conservation in blind children. *Education of the Visually Handicapped,* 1969, **1,** 101–105.

Miner, L. E. A study of the incidence of speech deviations among visually handicapped children. *New Outlook for the Blind,* 1963, **57,** 10–14.

Mungouan, J. F. More about retrolental fibroplasia. *American Journal of Ophthalmology.* 1956, **41,** 117–118.

Nissen, H. W., Chow, L. K., & Semmes, J. Effects of restricted opportunity for tactual, kinesthetic and manipulative experience on the behavior of a chimpanzee. *American Journal of Psychology,* 1951, **64,** 485–507.

Norris, M., Brodie, F. H., & Spaulding, P. *Blindness in children.* Chicago: University of Chicago Press, 1957.

Ohlmann, T., & Mendelsohn, P. Variabilite intraindividuelle des activites operatoires et dependance-independance a l'egard du champ. *L'Annee Psychologique,* 1982, **82,** 131–154.

Ohwaki, Y., Tanno, Y., Ohwaki, M., Harlu, T., Hayasaka, K., & Miyake, K. Construction of an intelligence test for the blind (Ohwaki Kohs Tactile–Block Intelligence Test). *Tohoku psychol. Folio,* 1960, **18,** 45–65.

Oi, H., & Maehigashi T. Experimental research on the process of solving "Tactile Block Designs Problems" by blind children. *Tohoku psychol. Folia,* 1956–57, **15,** 1–9.

Oleron, P. La perception tachistoscopique chez les sourds-muet. *Annee Psychol.,* 1950, **49,** 43–62.

Oleron, P. Pensee conceptuelle et langage. *Annee Psychol.,* 1951, **51,** 89–120.

Oleron, P. Role du langage dans le developpement mental: contribution tiree de la psychologie de l'enfant sourd-muet. *Enfance,* 1952, **5,** 120–137.

Oleron, P. Classement multiple et langage, *J. psychol.,* 1953, **46,** 299–315.

Oleron, P. L'education des deficients sensoriels. *La formation educative* (Pieron, H., *Traite de Psychologie appliquee*). Paris: Presses Universitaires de France, 1955.

Oleron, P. *Recherches sur le developpement mental des sourds-muets.* Paris: Edit. du C.N.R.S., 1957.

Oleron, P. Les activites intellectuelles. In Fraisse, P., & Piaget J., *Traite de Psychologie experimentale,* **VII.** Paris: Presses Universitaires de France, 1963.

Oleron, P., & Gumusyan S. Analyse perceptive et langage. Application d'une epreuve de Poppelreuter a des enfants sourds et entendants. *Psychol. franc.,* 1964, **9,** 47–60.

Oleron, P., & Herren, H. L'acquisition des conservations et le langage. *Enfance,* 1961, **3,** 201–219.

Omwake, E. B., & Solnit, A. J. "It isn't fair." *Psycho-anal. Stud. Child,* 1961, **16,** 352–404.

Parmelee, A. H. The developmental evaluation of the blind premature infant. *A.M.A. Journal of Dis. of Child.,* 1955, **20,** 135–140.

Parmelee, A. H., Fiske, C. E., & Wright, R. H. The development of ten children with blindness as a result of FR. *A.M.A. J. Dis. of Child.,* 1959, **98,** 198–220.

Piaget, J. Une forme verbale de la comparaison chez l'enfant. *Arch. Psychol.,* Geneve: 1921, **18,** 141–172.

Piaget, J. *Le jugement et le raisonnement chez l'enfant.* Neuchatel-Paris: Delachaux & Niestle, 1924.

Piaget, J. *La naissance de l'intelligence chez l'enfant.* Paris: Delachaux & Niestle, 1936.

Piaget, J. *La construction du reel chez l'enfant.* Paris: Delachaux & Neistle, 1936.

Piaget, J. *La psychologie de l'intelligence.* Paris: A. Colin, 1947.

Piaget, J. *Introduction a l'epistemologie genetique.* Paris: Presses Universitaires de France, 1950.

Piaget, J. Perception, motricite et intelligence. *Enfance,* 1956, **2,** 9-14.

Piaget, J. Logique et equilibre dans les comportements du sujet. *Logique et Equilibre.* Paris: Presses Universitaires de France, 1957.

Piaget, J. Assimilation et connaissance. La lecture de l'experience (*Etudes d'epistemologie genetique,* **V**). Paris: Presses Universitaires de France, 1958.

Piaget, J. Les praxies chez l'enfant. *Rev. Neurol.,* 1960, **102,** 551-565.

Piaget, J. *Les mecanismes perceptifs.* Paris: Presses Universitaires de France, 1961.

Piaget, J. Le langage et les operations intellectuelles. *Problemes de psycholinguistique.* Paris: Presses Universitaires de France, 1963.

Piaget, J. *L'Equilibration des structures cognitives.* Paris: Presses Universitaires de France, 1975.

Piaget, J. *Recherches sur l'abstraction reflechissante* (2 Vol.). Paris: Presses Universitaires de France, 1977.

Piaget, J. *Recherches sur la generalisation.* Paris: Presses Universitaires de France, 1978.

Piaget, J., & Garcia, R. *Les explications causales.* Paris: Presses Universitaires de France, 1971.

Piaget, J., & Inhelder, B. *La psychologie de l'enfant.* Paris: Presses Universitaires de France, 1966.

Piaget, J., & Beth, E. W. *Epistemologie mathematique et psychologie.* Paris: Presses Universitaires de France, 1961.

Piaget, J., & Inhelder, B. *Le developpement des quantites chez l'enfant.* Neuchatel-Paris: Delachaux & Niestle, 1941.

Piaget, J., & Inhelder, B. *La representation de l'espace chez l'enfant.* Paris: Presses Universitaires de France, 1948.

Piaget, J., & Inhelder, B. *La genese des structures logiques elementaires.* Neuchatel: Delachaux & Niestle, 1959.

Piaget, J., & Inhelder, B. Le developpement des images mentales chez l'enfant. *J. Psychol.,* 1962, **59,** 75-108.

Piaget, J., & Inhelder, B. Les images mentales. In Fraisse, P., & Piaget, J., *Traite de Psychologie experimentale,* **VII.** Paris: Presses Universitaires de France, 1963.

Piaget, J., & Inhelder, B. Les operations intellectuelles et leur developpement. In Fraisse P., & Piaget, J., *Traite de Psychologie experimentale,* **VII.** Paris: Presses Universitaires de France, 1963.

Plata, J. La sensibilidad tactil de los ciegos en relacion con la des los videndes. *Psicotecnia,* 1941, **2,** 158-175.

Plata, J. Sobre la relacion entre les conocimientos sensotactiels del ciego et los opticotactiles del vidente. *Psicotecnia,* 1942, **3,** 337-362.

Plata, J. La capacidad de los ciegos para la sintesis imaginativa espacial. *Rev. Psicol.,* 1948, **3,** 235-265.

Platner, H. *Philosophische Aphorismen.* Leipzig, 1793.

Revesz, G. System der optischen und haptischen Raumtauschungen. *Z. Psychol. Physiol.,*

1934, **131**, 296–375.

Revesz, G. *Psychology and art of the blind.* New York: Longmans, Green and Co., 1950. Translated from: *Die Formenwelt des Tastinnes,* La Haye: Martinus Nijhoff, 1933.

Riesen, A. H. The development of visual perception in man and chimpanzee. *Science,* 1947, **106**, 107–108.

Riesen, A. H., Chow, K. L., Semmes, J., & Nissen, H. W. Chimpanzee vision after four conditions of light deprivation. *American Psychologist,* 1951, **6**, 282.

Riesen, A. H. Effects of stimulus deprivation on the development and atrophy of the visual sensory system. *American Journal of Orthopsychiatry,* 1960, **30**.

Riesen, A. H. Studying perceptual development using the technique of sensory deprivation. *Journal of nerv. ment. Dis.,* 1961, **132**, 21–25.

Robertson, M. H., & Wolter, D. J. The effect of sensory deprivation upon scores on the Wechsler adult intelligence scale. *J. Psychol.,* 1963, **56**, 213–218.

Rosen, H. *Pathway to Piaget.* Cherry Hill, N.J.: Postgraduate International, 1977.

Rossi, P. L'adaptation psychologique de l'enfant au travail scolaire. *Enfance,* 1961, 403–421.

Rubin, E. J. *Abstract functioning in the blind.* New York: American Foundation for the Blind, 1964.

Seashore, C. E., & Ling, T. L. A comparative study of sensitiveness of the blind and seeing persons. *Psychol. Monogr.,* 1918, **25**, 108.

Senden, M. von. *Space and sight.* Glencoe-Illinois: The Free Press, 1960 (1st Ed. in German in 1932).

Siegel, A. I. Deprivation of visual form in the ring dove. *Journal comp. physiol. Psychol.,* 1953, **46**, 116–119.

Siegel, S. *Non parametric statistics for the behavioral sciences.* New York: McGraw Hill, 1956.

Simpkins, K. E. Development of the concept of space. *Journal of Visual Impairment & Blindness,* 1979a, **73**, 81–85.

Simpkins, K. E. Piagetian number concept in normal, retarded and blind children. Unpublished dissertation, Temple University, 1974).

Simpkins, K. E. Tactual discrimination of household objects. *Journal of Visual Impairment & Blindness,* 1979b, **73**, 86–92.

Smedslund, J. Apprentissage des notions de la conservation et de la transitivite du poids. *L'Apprentissage des structures logiques (Etudes d'Epistemologie genetique,*IX). Paris: Presses Universitaires de France, 1959.

Smedslund, J. The acquisition of conservation of substance and weight in children. *Scand. J. Psychol.,* 1961, **2**, 2–10.

Smedslund, J. Patterns of experience and the acquisition of concrete transitivity of weight in 8 years old children. *Scand. J. Psychol.,* 1963, **4**, 251–256.

Solomon, P., Kubzansky, P., & Leiderman, P. H. *Sensory deprivation.* Cambridge, Mass: Harvard University Press, 1961.

Spitz, R. A. Hospitalism. *The psycho-analytic study of the child,* **I**. New York: International Universities Press, 1945.

Stambak, M., L'Heriteau, D., Auzias, M., Berges, J., & Ajuriaguerra, J. de. Les dyspraxies chez l'enfant. *Psychiat. Enfant,* 1964, **7**, 381–496.

Steinberg, W. *Die Raumwahreneghung der Blinden.* Munich: Ernest Reinhardt, 1920.

Stephens, B. Glossary. In B. Inhelder, *The Diagnosis of Reasoning in the Mentally Retarded.* New York: The John Day Co., 1968.

Stephens, B., Gruce, B. *Piagetian approach to visually handicapped education. Phase II: Implementation.* Final Report, Project G00-78-01690. Richardson, Tx.: University of Texas, Dallas, 1980.

Stephens, B., Grube, C., & Fitzgerald, J. R. *Cognitive remediation of blind students.* Final Report, Project G00-74-07445. Richardson, Tx.: The University of Texas, Dallas, 1977.

Stephens, W. B., Piaget and Inhelder. Application of Theory and Diagnostic Techniques to the Area of Mental Retardation. *Education and Training of the Mentally Retarded,* 66, 1, 75-85.

Stephens, B., Simpkins, K. *The reasoning moral judgment and moral conduct of the congenitally blind.* Final Report, Project OEG-0-72-5464. Philadelphia: Temple University, 1974.

Stephens, S. Piagetian theory: applications for the mentally retarded and the visually handicapped. *Piagetian theory and the helping professions: the handicapped child.* Los Angeles: University of Southern California, 1977.

Sylvester, G. F. The mental imagery of the blind. *Psychol. Bull.,* 1913, 10, 210-211.

Thompson, W. R., & Heron, W. B. The effects of restricting early experience on the problem solving capacity of dogs. *Canadian J. Psychol.,* 1954, 8, 17-31.

Tobin, M. J. Conservation of substance in the blind and the partially sighted. *British Journal of Educational Psychology,* 1972, 42, 192-197.

Vernon, J. A., McGill, T. E., Gulik, W. L., & Landland, D. R. The effects of human isolation upon some perceptual and motor skills. In Solomon, P. *Sensory Deprivation.* Cambridge: Harvard University Press, 1961.

Vigotsky, L. S. *Thought and language.* Massachusetts: M.I.T. Press, 1962.

Villey, P. Les representations synthetiques des aveugles. *J. Psychol.,* 1930, 27, 391-411.

Vincent, M. Sur le role du langage a un niveau elementaire de pensee abstraite. *Enfance,* 1957, 443-464.

Wallon, H. *Les origines du caractere chez l'enfant.* Paris: Presses Universitaires de France, 1949.

Webster's Collegiate Dictionary. Springfield, Massachusetts: G & C Merriam Co., 1974.

Wechsler, D. *Echelle d'intelligence de Wechsler pour enfants.* Paris: Editions du Centre de Psychologie appliquee, 1959.

Weil, G., & Pfersdorff, C. Les fonctions visuelles de l'aveugle-ne opere. *Ann. med. psycho.,* 1935, 93, Part II, 367-382.

Wertheimer, M. Hebb & Senden on the role of learning in perception. *Amer. J. Psychol.,* 1951, 64, 133-137.

White, B. W., Saunders, F. A., Scadden, L., Bach, Y., Rita, P., Collins, & C. C. Seeing with the skin. *Perception and Psychophysics,* 1970, 7, 23-27.

Worchel, P. Space perception and orientation in the blind. *Psychol. Monogr.,* 1951, 65, 15.

Yong, M. L., & Harlow, H. F. Solution by rhesus monkey of a problem involving the Weigl principle using the oddity method. *J. comp. Psychol.,* 1943, 35, 205-218.

Zahl, P. *Blindness: modern approaches to unseen world.* Princeton: 1950.

Zubek, J. P. et al., Intellectual and perceptual changes during prolonged perceptual deprivation: low illumintion and noise level. *Percept. mot. Skills,* 1962, 15, 171-198.

Zubek, J. P., Aftanas, M., Kovach, K., Wilgosh, L., & Winocur, G. Effect of severe immobilization on the body of intellectual and perceptual processes. *Canad. J. Psychol.,* 1963, 17, 118-133.

Zuckerman, M., Albright, R. J., Marks, C. S., & Iller, G. L. Stress and hallucinatory effects of perceptual isolation and confinement. *Psychol. Monogr,* 1962., 76, 30 and 549.

INDEX

About the Author, Editor and Translator

Yvette Hatwell has, since 1973, been a professor of psychology at the University of Grenoble; in 1975, she established and became the director of the Laboratory for Experimental Psychology at Grenoble. Dr. Hatwell did her post-graduate work at the Sorbonne, where she worked with Jean Piaget, receiving her doctorate in psychology in 1965, and, in 1981 a further advanced degree for her work with Paul Fraisse. She has published extensively on the relationship between perceptual and cognitive development, and has worked on a variety of research and experimental projects on perception and tactual development in both sighted and blind children. She is at present at work on a book on space perception and visual-tactile integration in both children and adults, including both sighted and blind people.

Beth Stephens did her doctoral work at the University of Texas and postdoctoral work at the University of Geneva, and then served on the faculty at the University of Illinois, Temple University, and the University of Texas at Dallas (1965-1984). During this time she conducted research which utilized Piagetian assessments of cognitive development to analyze the development of reasoning in (1) normal, (2) mentally retarded, and (3) visually impaired pupils. Currently, Dr. Stephens, who is Professor of Special Education, the University of Texas at Dallas, is on leave to serve as Director of the Department of Dependents Schools, Alexandria, Va.

Pierre Verdet translated *Privation sensorielle et intelligence* into English while enrolled in the graduate program in Special Education at Temple University. This work provided information basic to Stephens' study of the development of reasoning in visually impaired pupils. Later, Mr. Verdet joined the staff of Vineland Training School, Vineland, New Jersey, and continued to work with exceptional pupils.